# REBUILDING the PAST

## A ROMAN VILLA

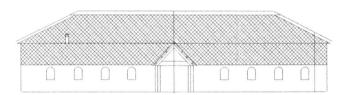

# REBUILDING the PAST

## A ROMAN VILLA

### DAI MORGAN EVANS

*with Christine Shaw and Roger James*

methuen

First published in Great Britain 2003 by
Methuen Publishing Limited
215 Vauxhall Bridge Road
London SW1V 1EJ

10  9  8  7  6  5  4  3  2  1

Published by arrangement with Discovery Communications, Inc.
The Discovery Channel logo and the 'Rebuilding the Past' logo are trademarks of Discovery Communications, Inc and are used under licence. All rights reserved.

A CIP catalogue record for this book is available from the British Library.

ISBN 0 413 77396 5

Printed and bound in Great Britain by Butler & Tanner Limited, Frome & London.

First page illustration: blueprint for Butser Roman villa by Tim Concannon.
Second page photograph: the build team at Butser Ancient Farm constructing the villa walls in August 2002.

# CONTENTS

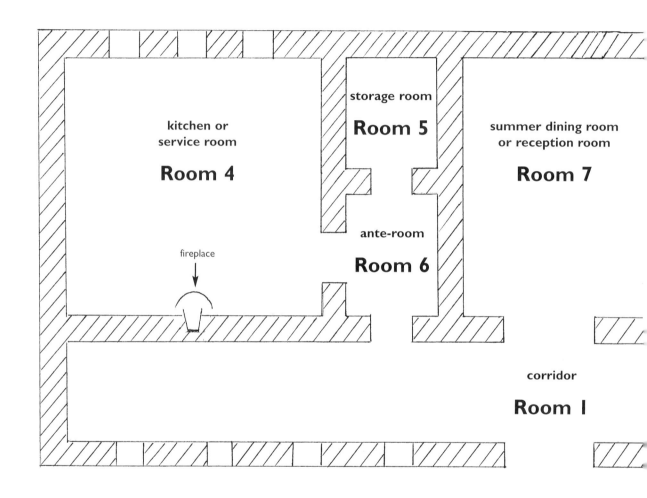

kitchen or
service room

**Room 4**

storage room

**Room 5**

summer dining room
or reception room

**Room 7**

fireplace

ante-room

**Room 6**

corridor

**Room 1**

1    2    3    4    5                    10

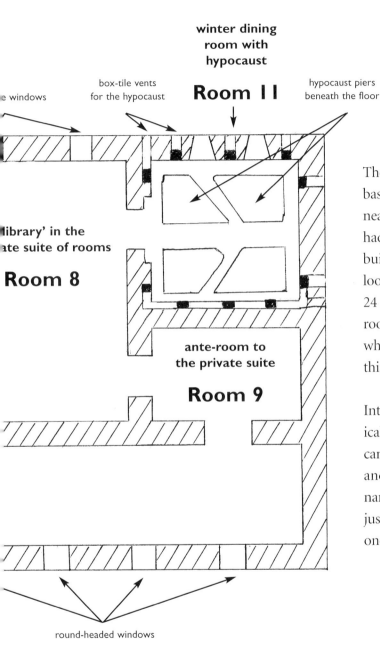

**winter dining room with hypocaust**

box-tile vents for the hypocaust

e windows

**Room 11**

hypocaust piers beneath the floor

**library' in the ate suite of rooms**

**Room 8**

**ante-room to the private suite**

**Room 9**

round-headed windows

The plans for Butser Roman villa are based on the villa found at Sparsholt, nearby in Hampshire. Sparsholt villa had two wings added after the original build, both with two rooms. If you look at the plan of Sparsholt on page 24 you can see that these additional rooms are numbered 2, 3, 9a and 10 which is why the room numbers on this floorplan are not consecutive.

Interpreting room usage in archaeological sites is a very difficult business, you can read more about it in Chapter 2 and throughout the book. So, the names given to rooms on this plan are just for convenience and only represent one of many possible interpretations.

**20**

**meters**

# ELEVATIONS OF BUTSER ROMAN VILLA

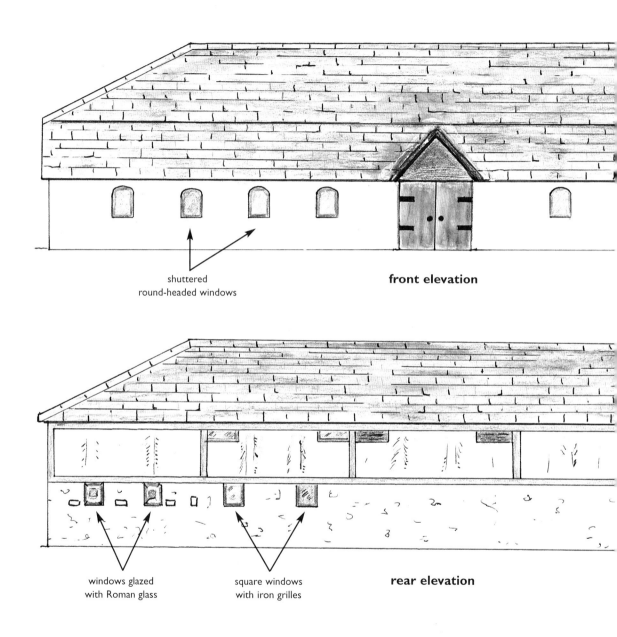

shuttered
round-headed windows

**front elevation**

windows glazed
with Roman glass

square windows
with iron grilles

**rear elevation**

3    6    9    12    15

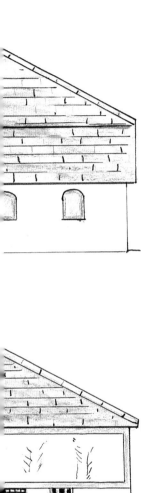

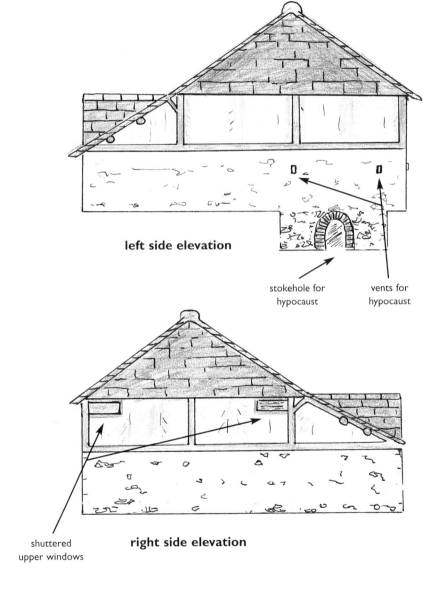

**left side elevation**

stokehole for
hypocaust

vents for
hypocaust

windows with clay,
and wood grilles

shuttered
upper windows

**right side elevation**

s

SHEENA — UNWAITH ETO LUSERN I FI

The excavation of the Sparsholt Roman villa, 1968.

# 1 WHY REBUILD THE PAST?

W hat do you need to build a house? Money and land of course, but even before that you need architect's plans of the interiors, elevations of the façades and details of services such as heating and plumbing. Then you require lists of what materials you will need and in what quantities. You also need to know that there are workers with suitable skills available to construct the building to a satisfactory standard and some sort of guarantee that it won't fall down when built. Then there is the whole question of 'location, location and location'. Is the land in a city, a town, a village or on its own in the country. All these factors affect the building and I haven't even whispered about the need for planning permission.

On top of this are all the assumptions that you make about the way of life that goes with the house. If it's a house rather than a bungalow then bedrooms are usually on the upper floors and the living rooms and kitchen are usually on the ground floor. If it's a bungalow, or a flat or a studio, all these assumptions change. Also, these days we tend to have some form of built-in central heating and often double glazing. We expect certain standards of comfort and recognise that we live our lives in the house or flat in certain socially accepted ways. Is it for a single person or is there a family in the house? Or has it reached the stage of 'empty nesters' or sheltered or supported housing? In older houses there are changes of expectation and technology since it was built. The 'front parlour' is no longer the recognised formal room, electric lights have replaced gas lamps, the outside earth closet has become the inside toilet and what was wrong with the tin bath in front of the fire? Having an inside bathroom loses a room! So building and occupying a house is part personal, part social and part technological. It can also be part historical.

If you want to attempt to build a Roman villa you have to face the same sorts of questions and problems – I'm going to put the question of modern planning laws to one side for now – but with the disadvantage that the factors listed above are often unknown. Also the Roman Empire was in Britain for around four hundred years (roughly the same as from now back to Shakespeare's times) and changes to local practices and customs obviously took place during that period. As you will see, we don't have the right plans and elevations; we know something, but not enough, about the materials and less about the workers; we are not too sure about the uses of the rooms and that's just for starters. Where we do know some of these factors they can be from places miles away from southern Britain where we want to build our villa, or from a different period to the building we are trying to recreate. Today we would not plan our buildings on examples from early nineteenth-century Tunisia – but those can be the sort of distance, time and climatic differences that we might be dealing with in searching for useful evidence.

Why is this so? The problem is that reconstructing the past from the study of the buildings and artefacts (in other words, archaeology) depends upon the state of the archaeological record. And if we want to use documents or pictorial evidence we need to understand their constraints.

## THE TROUBLE WITH ARCHAEOLOGY

What is the problem with archaeology? Look around you, even in today's world the materials that define your existence, comfort and

Cup recovered at the Sparsholt villa excavation in 1968.

lifestyle don't last for ever. We are a society used to disposables but it goes beyond that question. Think of what would happen to you and your surroundings if life as we know it stopped and the forces of nature got to work. Wood rots, metal rusts, flesh decays or, if you would like a more positive spin, all materials are all recycled in due course. And this is the problem with archaeology. What archaeologists have to deal with not only tends to be the material discards from life (or to put it more directly, rubbish!) but the structures we are looking at are ruins which have often been worked over. Think of abandoned houses – roofs disintegrate, either from lack of repair or by being stripped of slates or tiles for re-use, then the rain gets in, roof timbers rot, the place may be vandalised or stripped of useful materials such as fireplaces or lead and copper. The walls start collapsing as their timber rots and the place ends up as a mound of rubble which may then be taken away to use as hardcore. The process can either be slow and natural – but usually only in remote areas these days – or much quicker in areas where houses are being cleared for new developments. In the broadest sense, these are the sorts of circumstances that affect the remains that archaeologists try to make sense of. And if this happens to buildings and 'hard' materials, think of the effect on fabrics such as curtains or furniture – if there are any left once the house has

Waterlogged deposits provide the best circumstances for preservation as with the famous Lindow Man discovered in a peat bog near Manchester and kept in the British Museum.

been abandoned or cleared. The best circumstances for archaeological preservation tend to be waterlogged deposits such as peat bogs, riversides or the bottom of wells; or in places where it is very, very dry such as deserts. But these sort of places are not conducive to building houses and anyway, there are no deserts in Britain. However, we will be considering, in desperation, evidence from Roman Egypt and, a bit less drastically and closer to home, evidence of Roman timber buildings from beside the Thames in Roman London. So, however good modern technology and science are for archaeologists, say in terms of geophysics and pollen analysis, we can't improve on the basic surviving evidence.

Most of the time when studying the remains of a building the archaeologist depends upon evidence expressed as 'ground plans', the simple expression of the plan of a building. It may have the remains of floors but the walls do not stand high enough to deserve the title of 'elevation'. If the walls were built of decent stone then it might even have been 'robbed out' down to the foundations so the floor remains might seem to be surrounded by trenches. So we have some floors and some lower walls surviving but nothing over, say, one metre, which means no windows or details of the upper walls and no roofs unless the remains are lying in a jumbled heap. Metal artefacts, such as hinges, might be

Some Roman timber has survived in the wet conditions beside the Thames in London, this barrel is a good example from the British Museum.

present but they could be so rusted as to be unrecognisable. It also means, unless there are exceptional circumstances, that no wood or fabric remains so no doors, no shutters, no curtains and no leather hinges. And if you stop and think what that is in percentage terms, we are probably only ever dealing with between five and ten per cent survival of what was there originally, and that's on a good day! It's rather like trying to do a jigsaw with ten per cent of the pieces and, to help you, among them I'll give you fifty per cent of the straight edges so you can have some idea of the size. So, while a major part of the real excitement of being an archaeologist is piecing together the past it is also a hugely frustrating exercise and we need all the help that we can get.

When we look at the Roman period, the frustration of trying to work on the archaeological evidence is added to by the fact that while the Romans could (and did) write, they did not write about the things that interest us in building a Roman villa, that is, the minutiae of life. The Romans are quite good on history, poetry and propaganda but do not tend to bother with buildings. We have information from Roman literature about buildings but, to look at a more modern instance, try to reconstruct these houses and furniture from the diaries of Samuel Pepys:

> *To Clapham to Mr Gaudens . . . our first thing to show me is his house which is almost built . . . I find the house very regular and finely contrived, and the gardens and offices about it as convenient and as full of good variety as ever I saw in my life . . . it is true that he has been censured for laying our so much money . . . with good husbandry in making his bricks and other things, I do not think it costs him so much money.*[1]

This gives us dates for the building of the house and the fact that they were making bricks probably on or near the site but as for detail: what does he mean by *'other things'*?

So in this type of evidence, there are a few passing references which give some clues, but not enough to build up a detailed picture. This is because usually the details of buildings are not what the writers were interested in.

As you will see, we are slightly, but not much more fortunate with two of our Roman letter writers.

Can we learn from about buildings from Roman 'art' or pictures? There are few surviving because of the nature of the material, and those depictions that we have are stylised, idealised or may even be fantasies. Take a modern reproduction of Constable's *Flatford Mill*, more commonly known as *The Haywain*, as an example. The artist uses 'artistic licence' in representing the actual building to make it fit in better with his composition; certain detail is painted in a sketchy manner; the building itself is not the main subject of interest in the picture; the pigments that the artist used will have chemically changed over the years varying the colours and the modern reproduction which ends on the wall nearly two hundred years later will probably be smaller than the original, altering our appreciation of details. Bearing this in mind, we will need to remember that in Roman art the laws of proportion tend to be ignored; different kinds of perspective can be used in the same work or picture; the 'frontality' of façades or of people is important and art in general is traditional and conservative. So if we think of *Flatford Mill* in Roman terms the mill would be turned to make it quite clear that it was a mill with a waterwheel and if any of the people in the picture were at all important they would be enlarged and probably be presented face on; or *Flatford Mill* might be incorporated in a pastoral fantasy in a wall painting, which I suppose in one way it is. However, as we will see from the evidence of surviving Roman 'art', including sculptures, we do get some help as to how our Romano-British villa might have its walls decorated but there is not much help in considering the interpretation of the archaeological evidence.

PAST LIVES

To try and make sense of archaeological evidence, to experiment in how structures might have worked and to learn what questions to ask, we can try to 'reconstruct' buildings as a whole. Reconstruction makes us think in terms of actual buildings, not of ruins; of the complete not

Alan Sorrell''s
reconstruction of the
Llantwit Major villa.

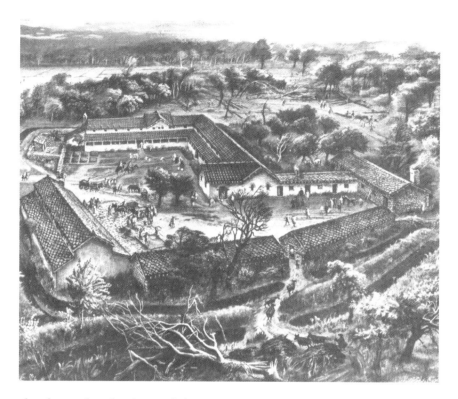

the decayed or broken; of the ninety per cent not the ten per cent. It makes us think in three dimensions, not in archaeological excavation plans and forces us to find answers to those questions we prefer to avoid or which, as archaeologists, we haven't even asked. The first, and cheapest, form of reconstruction is on paper or as computer graphics.

An early and very influential approach to looking at buildings and sites in three dimensions comes from the work of Alan Sorrell. In drawing his reconstructed buildings he carried out careful research on the ground plans, tried to make them work as standing structures and looked at the materials that would have been used, all based on the best archaeological evidence available. He was very keen on roofs and roof lines and this led him to draw from high viewpoints. Along with the first generation of television archaeologists such as Sir Mortimer Wheeler and Glyn Daniel, Alan Sorrell brought a whole new level of interpretation to the bits and pieces that archaeologists dig up. One of the first buildings that Sorrell 'reconstructed' was the Roman villa at Llantwit Major. This shows very well one

A fragment from the collapsed gable end of the Meonstoke aisled building which can be seen in the British Museum. The building was discovered in Hampshire, not far from Butser Ancient Farm. It shows us that round-headed windows were in use in Roman Britain as well as decorative pillars and tiles to make patterns.

of the important points that he made: a building does not exist in isolation. It is necessary to consider the building as an aspect of people in their environment. These people, he says:

> *will be enveloped in atmosphere, under a moving sky, shel-*
> *tering from a rainstorm or buffeted by the wind, and the artist*
> *will convince us that the ugly little stubs of wall, which are so*
> *often preserved as the final achievement of the archaeologist,*
> *are merely indications of what were once upon a time the*
> *dwelling places of people very much like ourselves.*[2]

Sorrell's work is important because his reconstructed images are so powerful that they have tended to dominate the imaginations and interpretations of many archaeologists. But while he has been very influential in this way, his plea for more accurate recording of how the archaeological evidence for structural collapse should be recorded, for example how roof tiles lie, has been largely ignored. Sorrell suffered, as all archaeologists have, in interpreting the archaeological evidence – and unfortunately that is from the lack of detail in published excavation reports, or from the fact that some haven't been published in any useful form.

A more recent approach to reconstruction drawing comes from Guy de la Bédoyère who has used the techniques of orthographic projection – the presentation of a three-dimensional object in two dimensions – and has considered the problems raised by the materials that the Romans had to hand. As he says:

> this does not mean that the reconstruction is right but that it is possible: a problem with beginning with an artistic interpretation is that one can unwittingly ignore a detail of the plan, making a restoration a technical impossibility. Orthographic projections force one to take note of the consequence of every feature of the plan.[3]

It is interesting in this case to compare Guy's reconstruction of the Llantwit Major villa with that of Alan Sorrell. One difference, which we will be considering again for our own villa, is how you treat the long low access room along the 'front' of the main building. Alan has it open as a sort of veranda, Guy has it closed in as a corridor but with several windows. Which one is right – and how can we tell?

The use of computer simulations has added another dimension. We can now 'move' through drawn line reconstructions and 'see' how parts might relate to each other. A good example of this is the work carried out by Julian Baum for David Mason on the enigmatic Roman site known as the 'Elliptical Building' in the Roman fortress of Deva at Chester. As David Mason, an experienced archaeologist, says:

> computer graphic skills have transformed the author's ideas about the superstructure and appearance of the Elliptical Building into photo-realistic images of high quality.[4]

This is a building which has been interpreted as a palace, gladiatorial school, theatre and market. The preferred explanation is that it was an *imago orbis terrarum*, a sort of representation, in building form, of the ancient inhabited world in a way which considers political and propaganda values. Not all experts agree with this, but the computer graphics do demonstrate the very special qualities of the building. However, in the end it is still just images on a small screen, and while we can intellectually engage with what is being proposed it is very difficult to really gain a sense of human scale and involvement. We observe rather than get 'in and amongst'.

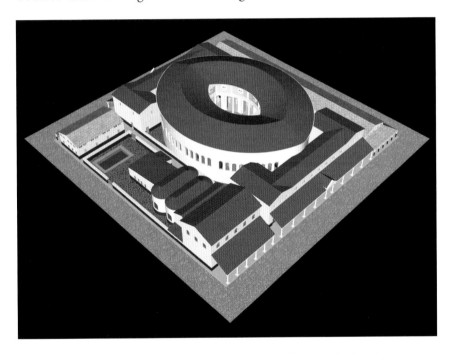

An image from Julian Baum's computer generated reconstruction of the Elliptical Building at Deva. You can find out more about this reconstruction, including images from the inside of the building at www.julianbaum.co.uk.

So while picture and computer reconstructions and simulations are very useful and give a form of 'reality' there is still no substitute for trying to build structures to full size using archaeologically authentic materials and techniques. The whole question of reconstruction comes in different ways.

Most ruins open to the public have been 'reconstructed' in some way to make them safe or even to save them. Most of the stones still standing at Stonehenge were reset in the first half of the twentieth century, if you look, and not so carefully in one case, you can see the concrete. But if this had not been done there would probably be, literally, only a handful of stones still upright. Tintern Abbey was also extensively rebuilt in the same period and there are many other examples. It is also possible to reconstruct a Roman building using breeze-blocks which are then plastered over and painted. This has happened at South Shields and gives some idea of what the Roman commander's house there looked like. As part of the visitor experience it has a role to play, but in some way it is a 'stage set' Roman building. This approach has a respectable history and can be seen at Cardiff Castle where, alongside the Victorian medieval interiors created by William Burgess, can be found a full-size Roman gateway built on the genuine foundations of a late Roman fort. But while it is interesting in many ways, this example tells us more about the Victorians than the Romans. A better approach is to maximise the information that you gain by building as authentically as possible. The Roman villa that we have built in this way at Butser Ancient Farm in Hampshire is an experiment which we hope has educational value.

## A TIMELY EXPERIMENT

An important example of the experimental process is the Experimental Earthwork Project at Overton Down in Wiltshire and Wareham Heath in Dorset. This is a pioneering experiment which was started in 1960 to investigate how sites, especially those formed of newly dug ditches and banks, 'decay' and change their form in becoming archaeological sites. Also within the earthworks a range of organic and inorganic material was buried to see how it changed and decayed. The change in the ditches, banks and materials is monitored by a series of excavations. The first plan was to excavate at intervals of 2, 4, 8, 16, 32, 68 and 128 years. Overton Down has had its thirty-second year excavation and Wareham Heath its sixteenth year. An important factor in choosing Overton Down was that it was on chalky downland while Wareham Heath is on an acidic heath. This affects the material buried in the sites in very different ways

Reconstructed Roman villa from Hechingen-Stein in Germany.

according to the chemistry involved. Bone tends to survive well in chalky soils so they are good for human skeletons or animal bones. However, chalk soils are not conducive to the preservation of pollen, so we might know that woodland was present but not what the types of tree were. Acid soils are bad for bones which get dissolved by the natural acid but they are good for preserving pollen, and this is very important as we will see when we look at the range of timber trees which would have been available for the Roman builders in Hampshire.

Short-term projects can also be important and interesting (even if they have nothing to do with the Romans). For example, the experimental reconstruction of the guns from Henry VIII's flagship, the *Mary Rose,* for the Royal Armories Museum tells us a lot about Tudor construction processes, skills and materials. As the guns were capable of being fired, we have learned about possible distances that they could fire and the damage they could cause to the enemy. The intervals required between firings to allow the guns to cool down and the number of people needed to serve the guns could also be estimated. We have learned that it is probable that the Nelson-era naval concept of one gun crew per gun is not valid for Tudor times and there could have been several guns served by one crew. However, even with a period so well documented (and, of course, we know everything there is know about the Tudors!), we still have a problem in that we do not know exactly what Tudor gunpowder was like. So while we can 'construct' a live firing test, we cannot properly 'reconstruct' one, but we do have a better idea about what is involved and we do recognise the constraints.

## CONTROVERSY!

It may come as a surprise, but the whole concept of trying to reconstruct the archaeological past causes a huge amount of ink to be spilt, ruins relationships between good friends and can all be very emotional. The key to this lies as much in the areas of sociology and psychology as archaeology but these tensions are a legitimate expression of people's attempts to grapple with understanding their past. The very word 'reconstruct' can upset people because it is said that in order to have a 'reconstruction' you have to have and know everything about the thing that you are reconstructing. So we can reasonably consider, for example, reconstructing the interior of 20 Forthlin Road, Liverpool, as it was when it was the home of the young Paul McCartney, and the National Trust have done just that. The information is available in the upstanding fabric of the building, in the living memories of the people who were associated with the place and in the fact that contemporary artefacts such as cookers and wirelesses still survive. In trying to recreate structures from archaeological sites the situation is very different. This is why the term 'construct' is used at Butser. I must confess that I think that it is more important to worry about the information and techniques that are used than to waste time worrying the words 'reconstruct' and 'construct' – oops, there's another friendship gone. The constructed

Building an Iron Age roundhouse at Butser Ancient Farm in Hampshire.

Roman villa at Butser is built using the best and most appropriate information available. But as you will see this information comes from a wide number of sources; means making interpretations and judgements and involves compromising with the modern world when it comes to planning and some matters of technology. In a very real sense it is an educational experience for those taking part and for those visiting because we had to relearn what the Romans knew first hand, and when it comes to the interior spaces, we are the first people for about 1,600 years to *feel* what its like to stand inside a Roman villa in Britain. This is a sensory and emotional experience as well as an intellectual one.

To get this *feeling* we believe that we need to build in materials that the Romans would have used. We need to understand and appreciate the techniques that were available to them and follow through the processes that we think they would have used. By building in this way we are being truthful in our approach to the building. But we are also experimenting, and we have to accept that experiments do not always work. This may be because we do not understand Roman techniques and we have to learn new lessons and see how old materials work together with a very practical 'suck it and see' approach. If we get it wrong, we have to go back to archae-ological evidence and see how it looks in the light of what we have tried to do. For example, in Chapter 5 we deal with the problems in interpreting a feature that could be a shrine or fireplace or hearth. We are not *sure* that we have the correct and final answer but we can see that it works in practice and we can use it to challenge the existing archaeological evidence. However, in the light of future excavations, we might find that we got it wrong – and we are not afraid of that. This is the nature of experimental 'constructs': we ask questions of the archaeological evidence, we find an answer or answers that are feasible and fit the evidence and we make the decision to build in a certain way. This method challenges archaeol-ogists to debate the issues with us, and in this way we advance our knowledge of ancient people and their buildings.

A late fourth-century picture of a country villa from the Bardo Museum in Tunis.

# 2 WHAT IS A ROMAN VILLA?

What is a Roman villa? This is the sort of obvious question which cries out for an easy answer. But there isn't one! First, we use 'villa' as a Roman concept, but we need to remember that Rome and its Empire lasted for hundreds of years and covered thousands of miles. So what might be true for a 'villa' in the first century BC in central Italy might be totally different for the late third century AD in southern Britain. Think of the way that the word 'hall' has changed its English usage from being a major part of a high status medieval building used for public display and sometimes feasting to a lobby passage from the front door sometimes used for storing bikes. Next, a Roman villa is generally understood to be a farm rather than a town house, but there are places called 'villas' which obviously are not farms – for example, Fishbourne in Sussex which is more like a palace. And then there are 'farms' which we would not call 'villas'. Iron Age roundhouses, like those at Butser, were farms and would have existed in Roman Britain, but no one would call these 'villas'. Villas generally should have 'status' building features like mosaics, hypocausts and painted wall plaster but there are sites which we would call 'villas' which barely fit this 'tick-list' of features even though the Butser Roman villa will show the expected range. There are the references to 'villa' in Roman law but these tend to be too simple. As a modern example, you can define a 'car' but the definition will not cover the range of types made since it was invented, nor its social or economic impact. So rather than spend more time on this, let us try our own modern definition: *A villa is a building with Roman attitude and of the Roman period set in the countryside.* What is meant by 'Roman attitude'? Well, read on, for most of this book is about trying to find out how we build in Roman fashion and with Roman attitude.

## THIS MUCH IS EVIDENT

When we look at the evidence from Roman buildings, not just villas, in Britain we find that very rarely are there any walls much over a metre high left standing. This contrasts strongly with military architecture from Roman Britain. For example, among the places you can visit are the later Roman walls of Chester still standing up to the wall–walk level, and there are tall defensive walls surviving at Caerwent in Monmouthshire, Silchester and Portchester in Hampshire, Richborough in Kent and other places. But as far as villas are concerned, most of the time the best we can expect is the bottom part of walls and often only the trenches where the walls have been robbed of their stone in later times. This makes it relatively easy to produce ground plans of Roman buildings and villas but very little else. Think of your own house if it was reduced to walls one metre high. You would have the plan and the floors. Details of the windows, even their locations would be lost. You would have the very bottom part of the door openings but no details of how they operated further up. Any wall recesses would be lost and as for the details of the upper part of the decoration of the walls, the ceilings or the roof – all this would be gone. So, archaeo-logically we can tell you a reasonable amount about Roman villa floors but not much above them. That is one of the reasons why mosaics attract so much interest: not only are they a form of art but they are the one surviving,

Detail from the mosaic floor at Sparsholt Roman villa.

relatively frequent, distinctive feature of 'Roman attitude'. Wall, and sometimes ceiling, plaster can survive in broken up fragments on the floor and in some cases, where a large section has come down, an area can be reconstructed. We are lucky that in a few cases the façades of Roman buildings have been structurally unstable and have fallen over. They can give an indication of heights, window positions and exterior decoration. One good example of this in Hampshire is that of the Meonstoke aisled building (alas, not a villa). A fragment of it can be seen in the British Museum in London showing the shapes of windows and the use of decorative pillars and tiles to make patterns. Besides this paucity of evidence there is the further problem of the robbing of Roman buildings for stones, tiles and other reusable material by later peoples. We call it robbing, but another way of thinking about it is recycling, or even sustainability, not that many archaeologists would be happy about the effects.

One Roman 'villa' which seems to be relevant was found at Redlands Farm, Northants. As with the Meonstoke building a gable end, in this case the rear one, had collapsed. The analysis of the fallen and standing masonry indicates that the total height would have been in the order of six and a half metres. The rear corridor wall was probably between two and a half and three metres. These figures are comparable with the Butser Roman villa. The main difference is that the Redlands Farm villa is in a limestone area, making it easier to produce coursed masonry, so it was built entirely in stone with no evidence of half-timbering like we have used at Butser.

## WHAT A VILLA ISN'T

We should briefly consider the question of Roman buildings that are not generally regarded as villas – although there are plenty of exceptions to prove the rule. To begin with we are ruling out as villas all the buildings found in towns or small settlements and all the building types found in connection with the military occupation of Britain. Given that Roman Britain was permanently occupied by a military force this excludes a lot of buildings. If we turn to buildings in the countryside we can rule out 'native-type settlements'. Romano-Britains continued to build 'houses' or 'huts' in the broad Iron Age tradition – such as the types we have reconstructed at Butser. And the fact that these buildings were round and thatched shows that they had not taken on board Roman building styles. Even when Roman style and attitude had been adopted there are strong regional differences within the Roman Empire reflecting local traditions, resources and, of course, climate. So in reconstructing our Hampshire Roman villa we have taken materials and techniques, as much as we can, from within the local area.

The large reconstructed Iron Age roundhouse at Butser Ancient Farm.

We then come to the type known as 'aisled buildings'. These are rectangular and the roof is carried on two lines of internal supports running parallel to the long side of the rectangle. These supports divide the interior space up into a central area and two smaller side areas or aisles. To us this would look like the inside of a church or rather like a large medieval barn. This sort of building is widespread throughout Roman Britain, it appears in conjunction with a main villa building and its use does seem to have been more agricultural. In some cases humans seemed to have shared the area with animals, a practice carried on in rural areas until comparatively recently. But the form and lowlier status of this type of building means that it is not called a 'villa'. Broadly speaking, this applies even to those aisled buildings which are developed and added to by means of subdivision of the interior into suites of rooms, sometimes with floors heated by hypocausts or with mosaics or, as with Meonstoke, elaborate facades. In the case of the villa at Stroud near Petersfield, not far from Butser, the aisled building had 'wings' added to it, so from the outside it would have looked like a winged corridor villa. So luxury features could be present and the aisled building could be disguised but it would still not be called a 'villa'. I warned you that the definition of a villa was not going to be easy and this is where 'attitude' comes in. The aisled building can be trying to be something that it is not but it will be found out. There is also a class of villas of such a size and complexity that we should call them 'palaces'. These include Fishbourne and Woodchester and, tempting though it is to pursue them, I shall refrain. They are too big, too complex in layout and with too many luxury features to really be called villas.

## BUILDING-UP

The sort of villas that we are dealing with are more like farm complexes today, some large and some small. The basic pattern starts with a 'corridor' villa, that is, there is a range of rooms to which access is gained from a common corridor. The corridor might

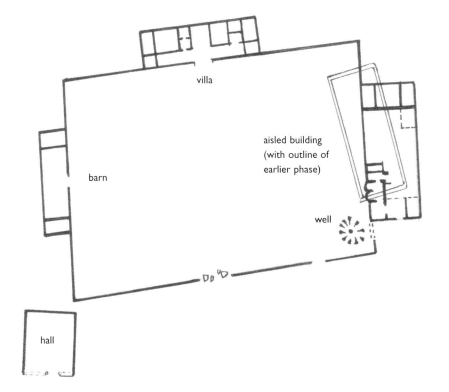

villa

barn

aisled building
(with outline of
earlier phase)

well

hall

have followed a Mediterranean style like an open veranda, perhaps with the lower part blocked in to form a portico. On the other hand, given the British climate it is probable that it was weatherproof and formed a long enclosed area, but we will be returning to this question when we consider the Butser villa walls. This basic design can be developed in a number of ways but the next major step was to add 'wings' at either end of the façade to form a 'winged corridor villa'. This is perhaps an example of Roman attitude making the façade more 'in your face'. This unit can then be developed further to take in separate or linked buildings to form courtyards. Not all the buildings around the courtyard need be domestic; indeed, given that the 'villa' is essentially a farm, we should not expect them to be. The complex at Sparsholt, Hampshire, from which the ground plan of the Butser villa is taken, shows several of the features mentioned above.

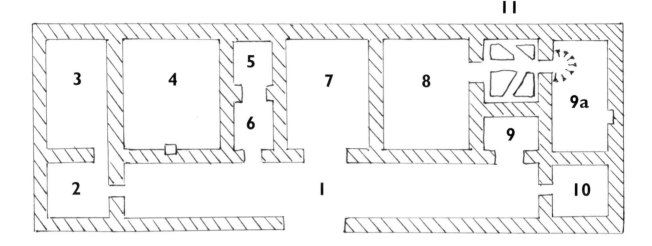

At Sparsholt, within the complex of a wall surrounding a courtyard, there is the main 'villa' building. It starts as a corridor villa then has two 'towers' added at either end. It is not quite a 'winged corridor villa' but it is moving in that direction. Part of the courtyard complex is an aisled building which was later divided up at one end with a mosaic tessellated floor laid in partitioned rooms. At the other end of the aisled building a bath suite was built complete with a vaulted ceiling. Within the aisled building there were also traces of a cooking area. Across the courtyard from the aisled building was some sort of storage barn. So the Butser villa needs to be seen as only part of a complex which will answer some of the questions about cooking, sleeping and bathing.

Detail of the villa part of the Sparsholt complex showing the room numbers assigned by David Johnston. It has two extra rooms on either side making it slightly larger than the Butser villa and explaining why the Butser room numbers are not consecutive.

### BUILDING BLOCKS

But knowing something about villa plans does not help us to learn where Romans building in Hampshire might have resourced their raw materials. Archaeology is also of limited help in this area. Flint is not a major problem as it can be found everywhere in most of Hampshire, as can limestone for lime mortar, but there is a problem with wood. We learn about the types of wood the Romans used either from actual wood found in acidic waterlogged deposits such as peat or from analysing the types of trees present in the area. This can be worked out from looking at ancient pollen but for this to be present we still need waterlogged deposits. Unfortunately, there is only one pollen sequence with Roman deposits in the whole of central-southern or south-eastern England and that is in Oxfordshire. In terms of firm evidence we are therefore in the dark. We can make reasonable guesses, based on other factors but these *are* guesses. The most helpful waterlogged deposits are all from London and will tell us a lot about the types of trees used and how the wood was worked but we have to be careful in using evidence from a big urban and port complex in constructing a small rural building on different geology.

## PICTURES OF VILLAS

We now turn to the representation of villas in pictorial form in Britain. A hopeful start might be made at the Brading villa on the Isle of Wight where there is a mosaic which includes the representation of a building. This building is in a central position on the mosaic panel and is therefore thought to have some importance. It has a pedimented roof with a finial at the front end and a rectangular doorway. The doorway is not a perfect rectangle but this is probably due to past repair and conservation, this reminds us to be careful about the interpretations we put on archaeological objects which may have changed since they were found. The building has a man with a cock's head standing near it. The Latin for 'cock' is *gallus* which is also a common Roman name and suggests that someone real and well known was being identified. It is just possible that the name was a pun on that of the emperor Gallienus (AD 351–354), which gives us an approximate date. On the other hand, it might be a representation of a 'fantastic' creature because, looking again at the decoration of the Brading mosaic, this central building is surrounded by different types of animals seeming to show a scene in an amphitheatre rather than a farm. If this is the case the building might be a small temple with steps

# Rebuilding the Past for the Discovery Chann

**IT** seemed like a dream commission. Katy Thorogood and Bettina Hatami at the Discovery Channel had asked us to produce a ten part series charting the construction of a Roman villa. There was only one problem: no one had built a Roman villa in Britain for 1,600 years.

A few days later I was doing what television producers do so well: picking other people's brains. That's how I came to be buying Simon West, Verulamium field archaeologist, a pint of best bitter in a St Albans pub. Simon seemed intrigued by the idea, suggested some contacts and said he would be supportive.

Three months later we began filming. Butser Ancient Farm seemed the obvious choice. Already an established centre for experimental archaeology, its team of resident archaeologists and enthusiasts had long dreamed of adding a Roman villa to their collection of roundhouses and had made a start on a hypocaust several years earlier.

So we had found an ideal site with an enthusiastic team and a hypocaust already underway. What could possibly go wrong? Well, just about everything. It soon became apparent that we had all seriously underestimated the enormity of what we had taken on; laying several hundred thousand flints by hand may be alright if you can round up a few dozen slaves but it was to prove an overwhelming task for Butser's small, inexperienced and under-resourced build team. The schedule slipped, we encountered the wettest autumn for twenty-five years, tempers frayed and the camera blew up. As the pressure increased, arguments broke out and people either left or were fired. The production team began to refer to the project as *Blood on the Terracotta* rather than *Rebuilding the Past*.

By Christmas 2002 it looked as if the villa was doomed and the television series along with it. We were in big trouble. I had spent a great deal of Discovery's money and Butser's reputation was on the line. Enter Dai Morgan Evans. I can best describe Dai as a realistic optimist. When he had agreed to become Butser's Chair of Trustees I suspect he had anticipated the odd meeting and a quiet life, but Dai quickly decided that he wasn't going to let Butser sink, so he pulled on his wellington boots and entered the fray.

Things began to look up and as the weather improved Christine Shaw was able to exploit one of Butser's great strengths as she recruited increasing numbers of volunteers to help finish the project.

What makes documentary filming so fascinating is that you hardly ever finish up with the film you thought you were going to make. Our original brief was to record an interesting archaeological experiment, but as things began to go wrong and the pressure increased we were able to film much more than the details of Roman building techniques. Our cameras were there as it gradually dawned on a small group of enthusiasts that they had taken on a much bigger challenge than they had realised. As they battled against the rain, the frost and the relentless grind of building by hand, they had to decide whether to cut and run or see the project through to the end. They stuck with it and built a villa. So in the final analysis, perhaps our series reveals as much about the tenacity of the human spirit as it does about experimental archaeology.

**Roger James** Executive Producer, Siguy Films

leading up to it. What it does not help us with is a depiction of a Roman villa close to our area.

While considering mosaics it is worthwhile briefly mentioning the extensive series of mosaics found in North Africa featuring what seem to be villa complexes. While these are interesting and we will consider some aspects of them again, they are not applicable to our case. These depictions are from a long way away and belong to a very different climate from that found in Britain. Also, the basic local culture and economy are not like that of Roman Britain so these mosaics do not help greatly. The same goes for the series of 'villas' depicted on the wall paintings at Pompeii, which not only date from over two hundred years earlier but in many cases seem to be showing 'fantasy' buildings and landscapes with plenty of 'artistic licence'. And bear in mind what was said in the last chapter about Constable's *Flatford Mill*.

Back in Britain, we have a graffito on the wall-plaster from Hucclecote of what looks like the gable end of a building. It has been interpreted as showing the half-timbering of an upper storey but equally it might represent something like the Meonstoke façade divided up by brick and tile. While this graffito is interesting we cannot

'Pliny the Younger and his Mother at Misenun' by Angelica Kaufmann. In this late eighteenth-century painting, Pliny is depicted dictating his famous letter about the volcanic eruption at Pompeii in which his uncle, Pliny the Elder, was killed.

use it as definitive guidance on the outside appearance of a villa – if that is what it is rather than, perhaps, an aisled building.

WRITING HOME

Can Roman documents help us? We have very few contemporary documents and because of the problems of archaeological survival they either come from very dry areas, like Egypt, or from wet areas, such as the 'wooden letters' from Vindolanda Fort on Hadrian's Wall. Unfortunately, none of these help us in our search for evidence. However, we do have some letters which have been passed down to us. The problem is that these letters have survived because they were thought to be examples of how letters should be written – public style is all important, even over content. They are not like Pepys's diaries: valuable because they were secret. But two of the authors of these letters are especially worth noting. The Younger Pliny (born about AD 61) describes his villa at Laurentium by the sea to the south of Rome as it was to him around AD 110.

> *It is seventeen miles from Rome so that it is possible to spend the night there after necessary business . . . The house is large enough for my needs but not expensive to keep up. It opens into a hall, unpretentious but not without dignity, and then there are two small colonnades, rounded like the letter D, which enclose a small but pleasant courtyard. This makes a splendid retreat in bad weather, being protected by windows and still more by the overhanging roof. Opposite the middle of it is a cheerful inner hall, and then a dining room . . . It has folding doors or windows as large as the doors all round, so that at the front and sides it seems to look on to three seas.*

Pliny then goes on to describe his bedrooms and then:

> *a room built round in an apse . . . and with one wall fitted with shelves like a library to hold the books which I read and read*

*again . . . The remaining rooms on this side of the house are
kept for the use of my slaves and freedmen, but most of them
are quite presentable enough to receive guests. On the other
side of the dining room is an elegantly decorated bedroom and
then one which can either be a bedroom or a moderate-sized
dining room.*[1]

Next, he speaks of the bath suite with its oiling room, rest rooms,
heated swimming bath and furnaces. Outside is the ball court, wine
stores and granary, more dining rooms and the garden. There is also a
terrace and arcade with another suite of rooms at the end where Pliny
can find peace and quiet when festivals are being celebrated in the
main house. Much of the 'working' of the buildings is to do with
enjoying the low sun, escaping the heat of the high sun and
maximising the effect of the cooling breezes. But this is a villa with
over forty rooms while our Butser villa only has eight. However, there
are themes that we will pick up again, for example, the flexibility of a
room that could be a bedroom or a dining room, and it is interesting
to see the concentration of this aristocratic Roman on the functions,
relative placing and views from the rooms of the villa. There is no
mention of decoration of the walls or floors and only one reference to
furniture when one of the rooms in his escape suite is said to be big
enough for a couch and two armchairs. But it has to be pointed out
that this large villa is over a thousand miles and around two hundred
years away from ours and, while it undoubtedly existed, we need to
remember that Pliny was writing for effect not for future villa builders.

The other letter writer who you will come across frequently in this
book is Sidonius Appolinaris. He lived in central southern France
near Lyons and Clermont-Ferrand from around AD 431 to AD 489,
at the time when the western Roman Empire was rapidly changing.
He will be quoted throughout the book on a variety of matters from
smoky fires to what happens when the bathhouses aren't working.
Sidonius, writing around AD 461, gives us a description of his
favourite villa at Avitacum, no doubt with the Younger Pliny in mind.

He first begins by describing his bathhouse in some detail including the decoration:

> *the interior walls are unpretentiously covered with plain white stucco . . . no frescoed scene obtrudes on its comely nudities, gracing the art to the disgrace of the artist. You will observe no painted actors in absurd masks, and costumes . . . with colours as gaudy as the rainbow . . .* [By the side of the baths] *you see in front of you the with drawing room; adjoining it is the store-room, separated only by a moveable partition from the place where the maids do our weaving. On the east side a portico commands the lake, supported by simple wooden pillars instead of pretentious monumental columns. On the side of the front entrance is a long covered space unbroken by interior divisions . . .* [from this] *the winter dining room is entered . . . a roaring fire on an arched hearth often fills this apartment with smoke and smuts . . . from here one enters a smaller chamber or dining room, all open to the lake . . . in its view* [then] *into a withdrawing room which in its coolness makes a perfect place in summer . . . a very small intervening chamber accommodates the drowsy servants, large enough to allow them forty winks but not a regular sleep.*[2]

He then goes on to describe his lake and the place where he plays ball. Unlike Pliny there is no reference to his gardens. Like the letters of Pliny we need to use those of Sidonius with caution.

And then there is Vitruvius, or to give him his proper Roman name, Vitruvius Pollio. Vitruvius wrote the Roman classic on architecture which is quoted in archaeological circles whenever the question of Roman building is discussed. For our purposes we need to note that Vitruvius was writing around 20 BC again in central Italy. His is a book of Mediterranean architectural styles and generally more concerned with public buildings than domestic ones, so most of it refers to temples, baths and public buildings, and very little is applicable to ordinary villas. However, there is a shorter version of Vitruvius dating to around AD 300 by Marcus Cetius Faventius which seems to reflect some actual experience and practice but, again, in Mediterranean areas. Sidonius recommends Vitruvius's work and that of a classic Roman agriculturalist called Columella as two 'musts' for a Roman villa- and estate-owning gentleman to have to read in the country. To me this smacks a bit of the two books on *Desert Island Discs* being the Bible and Shakespeare – well known classic works. But if they are available near Clermont Ferrand, why not near Winchester? So, we'll let Faventius have the last word on Vitruvius:

> *On proficiency in the art of architecture Vitruvius Pollio has written eloquently and at length with extraordinary knowledge. But for fear that their lengthy and erudite copious-ness may frighten less aspiring intellects off these studies, I have taken the resolution to clothe in everyday language a few items from their works, to be of use for private needs.*[3]

Of course he does no such thing, but the thought was there.

## THE MODEL VILLA

We now come to some 'model' representations of Roman buildings. From London we have what seem to be two model houses. They probably had some sort of religious function such as lamp holders. The model houses clearly have round-topped windows and it is suggested that the cross hatching carved out of the clay represents some form of timber framing. The cross hatching looks like that on the Hucclecote graffito. But these models, while apparently showing round-headed windows and perhaps some form of timber framing, are not really representations of 'villas' as far as we know them from the ground plans. At this stage one might start to despair but serious help is at hand.

The models which really seem to give us a clue as to what our villa really looked like come from Luxembourg – not so far away. Here were found some shrines carved out of single blocks of stone in the form of villas. They look very much like our corridor villas, with a clear break between the corridor and the main part of the building. They seem to show 'wings' at either end, making them 'winged corridor villas'. They also show square windows. All have the strong central element of a porch over the door with an inverted 'V' shaped pediment roof. Several show upper or 'clerestory' windows but one does not have this feature. The end walls have a triangular form. The roof is cross-hatched, perhaps indicating slates rather than tiles, and the end of one has marks on it, which could be interpreted as half-timber or painted decoration. These models give clear guidance (but not a set of detailed instructions) on form, but tell us very little about material. However, they do seem to reflect the ground plans we have in Roman Britain. So, while being far from perfect they give us the best and closest idea of what we should be aiming for in trying to build the Butser Roman villa. We need to accept realistically the types of information that we base the building of an 'authentic' Hampshire Roman villa on. It was a considerable challenge but, as you will see, we have tried to provide a reason for everything that we have done.

## PERSONAL SPACE AND PERSONNEL SPACE

Lastly, do we have any ideas on how the Romans might have used each of the rooms of the Butser Roman villa? Ideas yes, proof no. We know from documents that in general Romans thought of building space in terms of public and private areas and we know that Roman life was hierarchical (masters and slaves if nothing else) and involved certain 'ceremonials' which defined relationships. Vitruvius defines rooms such as bedrooms or dining rooms as 'private' and corridors and entrance halls as 'public'. To the public areas would come the employees or 'clients' of the villa owner especially for the morning *salutatio* or 'greeting' when they would affirm their reliant status and

One of the Luxembourg 'shrine' model houses.

perhaps ask for favours. The dining room would be for more intimate occasions, perhaps with social equals or those very close to the owner but would also be a place for formal social interaction. We should also bear in mind the unsolved problem of Roman family relationships. In

Wall painting of a rustic villa from a Roman town house in Trier, Germany.

Roman Britain there were extended families living together with the possibility of a greater role for women than in other parts of the Empire. We will be discussing the problems of room interpretation in greater detail, but here are two broad approaches you might like to think about.

One way of interpreting the use of the Butser Roman villa from its floor plan is as a central room with its entrance opposite the main entrance onto the corridor with two self-contained suites of rooms on either side. Both these suites have a similar arrangement of anterooms directly off the corridor and both have heated rooms, one by a hypocaust and the other by a fireplace.

This arrangement could be interpreted as a common public corridor and 'reception' room with two parts of a family on either side in self-contained 'privacy'. What the parts of the family were you can speculate – father and son and heir, matriarch and heir, brother and sister and their families, brother and brother and their families and so on.

Another way of looking at the floor plan is to identify the central room as the summer dining room with the wide entrance allowing a view across the corridor and out through the porch so that the estate landscape beyond could be viewed by the diners. It is also possible that the same room might double up as the public 'reception' room in the morning. If dining is what is important then the hypocaust room with its heating would be the winter dining room when comfort (of a sort) is more important. The room with the fireplace could be interpreted as the food preparation area. Part of this approach is determined by the suggested themes in the mosaics which might be seen to be associated with feasting.

The fact that two such radically different approaches to the use of the rooms considered shows the problems we have with interpretation. This is not to say that at one period the rooms were used in one of these ways and then a generation later in the other!

But that's enough theory, it's time to put our ideas about what makes a villa into practice at Butser Ancient Farm . . .

An Iron Age roundhouse at Butser Ancient Farm.

# ALL ROADS LEAD TO BUTSER

I t all started, in its present form, in May 2002 when Butser Ancient Farm was invited to build a Roman villa. The building project was to be shown on television and the approach, construction methods and materials were to be as authentic as possible. The challenge this project presented did worry the Butser people at the time but two things stood in their favour. First, as we shall see, they had already made a start on a Roman villa and secondly, they had experience of building in 'vernacular' materials including flint and lime mortar walls, timber roofs, and wattle and daub. This experience was clearly shown in the number and variety of Iron Age houses that had already been built on the existing site together with a small Roman grain-drying kiln built on the previous site that the Butser Project had occupied. When the invitation was received time was spent on estimating the amount of materials and labour that would be needed and checking that there were skilled enthusiasts available to deal with the practicalities of painting on wall plaster and laying mosaics. It was also hoped that significant numbers of volunteers would come forward to help with all aspects of the work.

The previous director of the Butser Project, the late Peter Reynolds, had made a start on a Roman villa on the site. This had got as far as choosing Sparsholt villa to act as a guide and laying out the ground plan of the rooms. A start had been made on the walls so that the plan was clear and work had taken place on the hypocaust room, including the masonry foundations for the floor supports and the walls up to one metre high, and the box tiles up to floor level – all this will make a lot more more sense once you have read the chapter on heating.

## NATURAL-BORN VILLA

The first question is why was the Sparsholt chosen as the 'model' villa? In choosing a site one was required that would fit into the area, use local materials, and be 'native' to Hampshire – not that the county existed in Roman times, although some of the Roman administrative boundaries may not have been that different. The credibility of the villa as a construction depended upon this local identity and it is something that we have worked hard at, not always successfully. So Sparsholt villa was 'local'. It had been excavated from 1965 to 1972 by David Johnston, an archaeologist specialising in the Roman period, including reconstructions, who was on the staff of Southampton University. The excavations showed that there had been a complex of buildings around a courtyard which had a formal entrance. There was also an aisled building with an associated bathhouse, a barn, and then the main 'villa' building. It is this main building that we have used as the basis for our construction of the Butser Roman villa. The Sparsholt villa was built with flint and lime mortar, it had been roofed with Purbeck stone tiles and it had mosaics, tessallated floors, and *opus signinum* floors (see the chapter on flooring for explanations of these). Its floorplan – a corridor villa – also posed all sorts of questions about how the rooms were used, what social implications could be read into them and so on. We have dealt with some of these questions in the previous chapter. The Sparsholt villa contained many challenges of interpretation but it was not too big. It was more representative of the smaller to medium-sized Roman villas rather than one of the 'palaces'. One of the personal touches of this project is that it was Professor Martin Millett, then at Southampton University, now Professor of Classical Archaeology at Cambridge, who recommended to Peter Reynolds that Sparsholt was the example to use as a guide.

Roof tiles frome the Sparsholt villa site, the black and white scale in the centre shows the size in centimetres.

## A LEVEL PLAYING FIELD

So it was agreed in June that a villa based on Sparsholt would be constructed. And it would have a flying start because some of the more complex work had already been done – in fact it was agreed to undo some of the work on the hypocaust to help the explanations needed for the programme. Work started in mid-July with the intention that the villa would be finished in the autumn, a time-span of about four months. At this stage how about a word from the Roman writer on architecture and building?

In hindsight Vitruvius has some prophetic words about starting the construction of a Roman villa:

> *But when I see that the importance of such a great profession* [of architect] *is arrogated by the ignorant and inexperienced, and by those who not only lack knowledge of architecture, but even of construction technique, I cannot but praise the heads of house-holds who, trusting in their own reading, build for themselves in the belief that, if they entrust a commission to amateurs, they themselves are more worthy of the expendi-ture, which will be according to their own wishes rather than those of others.*

This, explains Vitruvius, is:

> *why I thought that I should record the body of architecture and its governing principles as thoroughly as I can, thinking that this will be no unwelcome gift for all nations.*[1]

The villa site in August 2002, levelled and ready for building.

But while we were not entirely 'ignorant and inexperienced' the late summer and autumn of 2002 were, in summary, a period of continual difficulties – all right, disasters – for the Butser Roman villa project.

The first thing to go wrong was the discovery that when the Butser villa had been laid out the levels had not been properly assessed and it was built across a slope. If the villa had been built at the level set by the hypocaust room floor, the floor levels at the other end of the building would have been a metre above the existing ground level. This is too steep a slope over the length of the building to allow for 'natural' internal slopes, especially in the corridor. It did not seem appropriate to have internal steps within the building and there is not much archaeological evidence for this. To

The new hypocaust, mid-construction in September 2002 looking more like an archaeological site than a building site.

produce an internal level surface would mean importing and consolidating a lot of material inside the building. This would also have the effect of lowering roof, door and possibly ceiling heights especially in rooms 5, 6 and 7 as well as the adjoining corridor. Alas, there was no alternative to demolishing the existing work, especially the hypocaust room and dig out this end of the site by one metre to produce a level platform. This was after the project timetable had already begun and also meant rebuilding what had been started and what had been assumed would give the project its flying start. About five weeks were lost due to this change of plans and this was in a project with a twenty-week schedule. The first flint of the 'new build' was laid on 13 August 2002.

## UP AGAINST THE WALL

The next major problem was the rate of build for the flint and mortar walls. This had been hopelessly underestimated. While not making

## Rome Wasn't Built in a Day ... by Simon Jay build team member

**I BECAME** aware of the intention to build a Roman villa at Butser when Jonathan West who was the educational officer of the ancient farm contacted me. He explained that they required skilled personnel who were prepared to offer complete commitment and dedication to the job. After an interview at the farm, I knew immediately that I would like to be involved and I accepted the job.

We started slowly because everyone's efforts went into the structural walls and later there were several weeks of very wet weather. Although I have always been optimistic about the project, halfway through, when the weather and other difficulties brought work to a halt, I began to have some small doubts that the villa would ever be finished. But due to the dedication of the management team, especially Christine, we pulled through.

As soon as the walls were completed the roofing timbers arrived. My previous experience in forestry meant that I appreciated the work that had gone into shaping the raw timbers, and later I was able to use my skills to cut hundreds of hazel rods from local woodland to use in wattling.

During the past year I have enjoyed every day: the laughs, the challenges and the new friends, plus I have learned a great deal about the Romans. I believe this must be the finest replica Roman building in Britain and I feel proud and privileged to have been part of such a grand project. Hopefully this will just be the start of other similar ideas.

excuses, there are not many people around who build flint and mortar walls in this fashion. Most contemporary flint walling consists of a facing 'skin' on other materials such as breeze block or brick. Butser had some experience in flint walling, but this was on a modest scale and did not, in retrospect, prepare the project for a far larger scale and more pressured timetable. Under pressure, several efforts were made to produce a realistic build-rate, but none proved satisfactory. The result was that by late October only about ten per cent of the wall had been built. Other factors then started to come into play, such as the weather. The way that the wall was built followed the example of the Sparsholt villa. It was said that this style was essentially of a flint dry-stone wall. Dry-stone walls stand because the size, shape and weight of the stones interlock to form a sound structure. They need no bonding or 'gluing'

41

medium such as mortar or cement. It was said that the Sparsholt style of
flint wall only needed the mortar to fill in the gaps and to provide a small
bit of stability and strength. As we will see, the mortar used at Butser was
made of lime, and this type of bonding agent only dries comparatively

Early days building the
flint walls, August 2002.

slowly – especially compared to modern cements. However, on a true
'dry-stone' basis the wall could be built almost whatever the weather.
Unfortunately this did not prove to be the case. The lime mortar proved
to be an essential part of providing the strength and stability of the walls

as they were being built. Therefore, we had to obey the weather and seasonal conditions under which lime mortar set. Wise after the event? Remember what was said in Chapter 1 about taking archaeological observation and experimenting with it? Perhaps we got it wrong because the lime mortar content of the Sparsholt walls had been reduced by natural causes meaning that incorrect (as it turned out) observations were made? Whatever – the wall build was way behind schedule.

## PLANNING PERMISSION

The next problem was the roof. This proved a problem at this stage because the height of the walls depended upon the design of the roof and *vice versa*. The plan adopted for Butser following Sparsholt has a corridor the length of the building with rooms off of it. The excavated walls were all of the same thickness so you can have one roof for the main part of the building and another adjoining roof for the corridor which is the solution we adopted. On the other hand you could go for a roof which covers both the main block and the corridor in one span. This means that the highest point (the ridge) runs down the middle of the whole building rather than down the middle of the main block. To build this

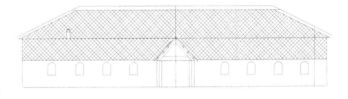

Tim Concannon's villa blueprint which was eventually granted planning permission.

'one-span' roof as proposed meant carrying the flint and mortar walls up to a general level of two and a half metres with a maximum of nearly five metres to carry the top of the roof and with a corresponding equivalent increase in height for the inner corridor wall and other walls. No half-timber solution was considered. While there is no doubt that this roof would have worked, it had one major problem as far the timing of the project went. This height of walls needed to be worked off higher scaffolds, so this would increase the time taken to build the walls and, most importantly, it would need the firm setting of the lime mortar with the flint in order to carry the weight of the wall above.

Building the new hypocaust, August 2002. Note the large piles of flints waiting to be sorted.

There was also the need to gain planning permission. It had been thought that there was permission to build the Roman villa as part of the permissions given for the site including the Iron Age houses. This turned out not to be the case. Planning permission was duly applied for. Whichever way you look at it, the Butser Roman villa is a new building, however 'old' the concepts behind it. Have you ever tried to apply for permission for a new building in what is an Area of Outstanding Natural Beauty, and – it's a big 'and' – an area which will shortly become England's first National Park for some time and the first one in the south-east? To cut the story short, the planners were sympathetic to the aims of Butser, especially the educational ones, but wanted a 'new' building that would blend into the countryside. In one way, the more it could look like a 'vernacular' non-residential building, the better. In particular, this affected the height of the building which had to be a maximum of six metres. We are not griping about the planners, and they

44

have been very helpful within their constraints, but if you have a desire to build a Roman villa remember that the law has changed since Roman times, and nobody is going to actually live in this villa.

## WHATEVER THE WEATHER?

So we had a project with planning permission and on level ground but badly behind schedule. We were conscious that the weather would become colder and it became more urgent to think how we could get a covering over the villa area to allow work to continue in the winter months – that is, put the roof on. A compromise was worked out which would allow for temporary 'modern' piers to be put in to support the roof, which could then be replaced later. As this became less feasible it was agreed that we would try to complete the walls of about half the villa so as to allow work on part of it to proceed during the winter months. Even

Work continued on the walls into the autumn but had to slow down in mid-October as the weather became colder and wetter.

this was not to be. From the autumn the weather became increasingly wet and cold, making real progress on the project almost totally impossible. The rain poured down continually, making this the wettest October, November and early December for thirty years. The heavy rain started in mid-October. There were four inches of rainfall in the second half of October, eight and a half inches in November and five and a half inches in December. Not only did the weather affect the rate of work, it also affected the materials. It became apparent that the lime mortar was not setting fast enough and that if work continued the lower parts of the walls would not bear the weight of the later work and would bulge – which could lead to 'slumping' where the wall collapses. In order to keep some work continuing a marquee was hired so that the lower parts of the walls could be built up under cover and with some protection from the cold. The marquee meant that the build rate was extensive for area rather than intensive for height, which reduced the risk of slumping because the walls were only taken up as far as was deemed safe and then left. This period did allow the calculation of realistic build rates, including the preparation of the materials and most efficient ways of working.

At Christmas 2002 it was decided to slow the wall building right down, rethink the project archaeologically and plan for the next building season which, for working in lime mortar out of doors, would start in March 2003 at the earliest.

BACK TO BASICS

The process of assessing the Butser Roman villa project went back to first principles. In a way, it gave us time to think, which had not been available back in June 2002. In its underlying academic principles the project owes a huge debt to Professor Martin Millett who greatly assisted with our rethink. Having pointed Butser in this direction years ago when he recommended the Sparsholt model, it was very good that he was able to keep prodding it! While his input has been crucial it is only fair to say that the responsibility for what has been built entirely lies with the project directors and the build team.

We started again from the ground plan that was partly built up, in sections, to window height. Using the existing roof design, with one span for the entire villa, meant that while there was a satisfactory appearance from the outside, when we came to imagine how the main rooms would look from the inside, it seemed to us that it would make the shapes very irregular with no internal symmetry. It just felt wrong to be thinking of standing at the back of the main reception/summer dining room and having the highest part of the room off-centre to the front and a high wall

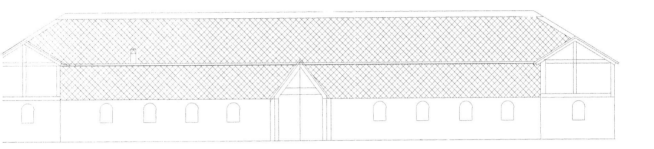

above the door with the side walls not forming a regular shape. I suppose that if we go for single span roofs over corridors that is the logical option, but given our understanding that in some circumstances Romans favoured symmetry it just did not feel right.

As it happened, when we came back to what we really know about the appearance of Roman villas – and you have already seen how little that is – the Luxembourg 'shrine' models gave us the approach that we decided to follow. So that gave us the broad principles to follow for the external appearance with essentially two roofs, one over the main block and a 'pentice' or 'cats-slide' roof over the corridor. This would also solve the problem of symmetry in the main rooms as the ridge and highest point would be over the centre of them.

Tim Concannon's blueprint showing added wings like those of the Sparsholt villa.

Following the Luxembourg shrine models produced a new problem. We had changed the roof line so it would be necessary to go back to ask for a change of planning permission. Following some of the models, we also asked if we could have 'clerestory' windows, that is, a line of square or rectangular windows, above where the sloping corridor roof meets the main block. The purpose of these windows, we think, is to give light to the main rooms from the front of the building to add to the light from the rear. There were two practical problems with this approach. The first is that the height of the villa would have to be raised by another metre from the existing agreed six metres to give extra wall space and this would take the building above the height which is felt appropriate for agricultural buildings. The second point

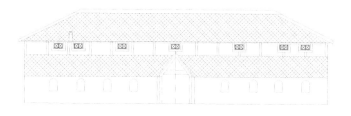

Tim Concannnon's blueprint showing an upper row of 'clerestory' windows.

was that putting 'upper' windows in was felt to make it appear to be a two-storey building and this was unacceptable to the planners. Ironically, this reflected some of the arguments currently going on about whether Roman villas were one or two storied. So we were given permission for the changes to the roof within a maximum height of six metres but no upper windows. In fact one of the shrine models appears to show this situation.

The next major decision was whether to make the upper part of the Butser Roman villa timber-framed. You will come to the discussion of this later on. The decision is frankly experimental but allows various theories about the construction of Roman villas to be tried out and also gives added educational value to the villa by demonstrating different building techniques.

There were also the broad decisions to be taken about the nature of the floors. In a way this is where the real changes take place from the Sparsholt villa. We took the decision in principle that we would try out and display the range of flooring types that could be reasonably be expected to be found in a villa in central southern England. But, while we spent the first two and a half months drawing up work schedules and getting the broad picture, this is not a routine or repeated building project for which you can produce an exact specification. However, we did construct a schedule taking the project up to the end of September.

Work on the flint walls started again in mid-March with the experienced, and remaining, members of the old build team. The work rate had been sorted out and a schedule of work to be completed within set times drawn up. This could be adjusted as necessary. The result was that the wall was completed on schedule and within budget by mid-May. It might be rather boring to report this after our previous trials but it shows what informed scheduling can do and it did depend utterly upon the enthusiasm, dedication and sheer hard work of the build team and the regular volunteers.

The project was also very fortunate to gain the services of Ian Pritchett and Robin Flowers who are involved with timber and other vernacular building techniques. They had not tried anything Roman before and it was often quite clear that the rougher aspects of Roman techniques pained them greatly. However, they were prepared to sacrifice their standards of craftsmanship in trying to achieve Roman authenticity. Their experience and professionalism meant that the upper part of the walls and the boarded roof structure were erected on time and on budget (you can read about the roof in Chapter 6). While August 2003 happened to produce a heat wave rather than heavy rain, the presence of the roof meant that work on the interior could carry on whatever the weather and could be planned in. So work on wattle and daubing (Chapter 4), the floors and mosaics (Chapter 7) and the wall paintings (Chapter 8) could all continue to the end of the current phase of the project.

From the beginning of the year onwards a great deal of research was going on into the other details of the Butser Roman villa, about windows, shutters, doors, ironwork and so on. You will find the challenges that determined how these looked discussed in Chapter 9. In a very real sense this research work has continued throughout the current programme of building the Butser Roman villa as new problems have arisen or suggested solutions don't work or seem right. This research and the experiments will continue well into the future.

The villa in May 2003. The Flint walls have been built and await plastering.

# 4 THE BUILD TEAM GO TO THE WALL

To begin at the very beginning: how did our villa owner choose of his site? Vitruvius and Faventius gave the following advice: 'You must take care, then, not to make doors or windows that face harmful winds . . . winds do harm either when they are too strong or when they bring cold so bitter that it harms men and animals. In cold districts you must place your doors and windows so that they face south . . . while in hot districts you must contrive that they face north . . .'[1] But in some cases, as at Sparsholt, the presence of earlier buildings dictated the positioning of the new block – or perhaps the villa was planned from the very start.

Another important factor appears to have been the presence of water, although in the case of the Great Witcombe villa in Gloustershire, the site chosen was on a hillside with streams and springs running down it, making for potential and actual problems with damp. As we saw with the quotes from Pliny and Sidonius in Chapter 2 the question of summer dining rooms having a good view also appears to have been important. So 'location, location and location' appears to be a very old concept!

Having decided the site, what next? Commission a surveyor and an architect? There is evidence for both in the Roman world – Vitruvius and Faventius make that clear and we did have some in Britain. But these seem to be mostly military personnel or people associated with military works. There is no doubt that the appearance in Britain of the Roman army with its building professionalism and skills would have greatly changed and influenced local buildings techniques. While building in a town might have been hedged around with all sorts of laws and regulations (yes – even then), it is probable that our villa owner, building on his own land and utilising to a large extent his own resources, would not have had to worry about many constraints, except perhaps that of the 'real' cost of the resources: can you take people from working the land to help build a villa when the best agricultural and building periods coincide? Guy de la Bédoyère neatly sums up the situation in a way that could equally be applied to the 'self-build owners' that Vitruvius identified:

Measuring out the walls
Roman style, August 2002.

*Many Romano-British architects belonged to the 'suck and see' school of thought, contrasting with the popular image of Roman building as the product of competent planning and techniques. In other words if the building started falling down it was either patched up or abandoned. If it didn't fall down there wasn't a problem. If correct this suggests that successful projects were as much a result of luck as design.*[2]

So, buildings were 'designed' by an 'architect' of some sort, or, more often, just by the owner and surveyed in by various means. There is an extensive literature on Roman surveying instruments and the length of Roman 'feet' – there was more than one standard and they vary internally in themselves. Also there are discussions on whether these 'feet' can be identified as units in existing Roman buildings. But, by the end of the surveying process, the villa owner has (or thinks they have) the resources to build an idea of what they want to build and the outline is there on the ground. So we are now ready to start on the wall.

## THE WALLS FROM BOTTOM TO TOP

To start at the bottom: the walls of the Butser Roman villa follow the archaeological evidence from the Sparsholt villa and do not have foundations as such. The wall is set directly on the chalk platform and built up from that point. There are good reasons for this. The native chalk lies close below the surface and provides a solid base from which to work. If we had been in a deeper soil, on clay or in 'made ground' – such as an earlier ditch – we would have put in deeper foundations as appropriate. The other thing we have not done is to put in any sort of damp course to stop moisture travelling up through the wall, or indeed under any of the floors. There was no archaeological evidence for this at Sparsholt and we are also aware that walls made, like ours will be, with lime mortar 'breathe' of their own accord. From Vitruvius and Faventius we are told that the Romans had their own methods of curing walls which were too damp and this was not with a damp-proof course in the wall:

> If continuous damp seeps through them, for three feet from its foot you are to clothe your wall with baked earthenware and then pound and polish this lining, so that it will be impervious to damp. But if there is a larger quantity of continuous damp, you will build a short channel, rather below the level of the floor inside, where the water can collect and run away without endangering the wall. But if a great quantity of water wells up, you must carefully spread pitch over the two-foot tiles at the place where the water breaks out of the wall, so that no moisture may force its way into the structure of the wall.[3]

Faventius then adds that these tiles must be strongly cemented to the face of the wall. So if we have a damp problem we know how to cure it. We will also be providing a drainage channel around the Butser Roman villa to take away water from the roof – the Romans did not have gutters and drainpipes.

Looking at the Butser villa you might be puzzled as to why the walls are so wide given the relatively small area that the timber framing occupies on top. Surely the walls could have been narrower? The width of the walls is based on the excavated villa site at Sparsholt and it is worthwhile noting that they are the same thickness throughout the villa. If the walls were built to reflect their load-bearing capability this would be curious as we would have expected thinner walls to the exterior of the corridor. Or if the roof structure was carrying the load onto the outer walls of the villa (including the corridor) why were the inner walls not thinner? We do know that Roman walls could be built to reflect different needs. The gable end at the Meonstoke aisled building was made thicker than the side walls, presumably because it was carrying more of the roof load. So we need to think of an explanation for the uniform thickness of the Sparsholt/Butser walls.

While we have gone for a timber-framed structure for the upper part of the walls, there are other possibilities. One is that the walls could all have been carried up to roof height in flint and lime mortar – the gable ends would have been in flint as would the upper side walls. But another possibility, which explains the thickness of the walls, is that they might have provided a base for the upper part of the structure to be made of an earth-based material such as cob (a mixture of puddled clay and chalk together with straw). This was a technique being practised in Hampshire in the late eighteenth century. Gilbert White was a famous Hampshire naturalist based in Selborne. His description of a house martin building its nest of mud and straw says:

Uncovering the flint walls of the Sparsholt Roman villa, 1970.

*Then, that this work may not, while it is soft and green, pull itself down by its own weight, . . . has prudence and forebearance enough not to advance her work too fast; but by building only in the morning, and dedicating the rest of the day to food and amusement, gives it sufficient time to dry and harden. . . . Thus careful workmen when they build mud walls (informed at first perhaps by this little bird) raise but a moderate layer at a time, and then desist; lest the work become top-heavy, and so be ruined by its own weight.*[4]

An alternative to cob is to build in mud brick. These are bricks made of earth, tempered with straw or grass and allowed to dry. Both these earth-based walls would be coated in lime plaster and lime-washed to make them weatherproof. The great advantage of having these materials on a high stone base is that they will not weather away at their weakest points which is the effect of rain splash at ground level. The other weak point is at their tops if the rain and frost get in. But these tops should normally be protected by the roof and these earth structures do have load-bearing strength. However, if they existed on a site it would normally be difficult to prove because when they erode and decay they become a featureless heap of earth no different from the ground which they came from and it is difficult to prove things one way or the other. We have a similar problem if the walls were raised to their full height in flint. While we might hope that if the building collapsed we would be able to estimate its height from the quantity of flint on site, the provision of a large pile of building material would be very convenient for later builders. This means that on most sites the building material has been 'recycled' and taken away. This makes it impossible to calculate the heights of walls from the materials left on the site. All of which brings us no nearer to a definitive answer to why all the walls are built so widely.

We can only fall back on the irrational. Nowadays, structural engineers know the loadings of walls, but in Roman times they seem not to have had the ability to calculate such things. So it is suggested that the villa walls were 'over-engineered' to allow a major safety margin. If the materials and labour were cheap then it made little difference to build the walls wide and all the way round with no partic-ular thought of what the walls were meant to do. The fact that the corridor wall is built in this way particularly inclines me to this view. At one stage we had considered that the thickness of the walls might be a deliberate form of insulation – cool in summer, warm in winter. However, although the insulation properties of wattle and daub are said to be quite good, we will have to wait for winter to see how the half-timbered upper part affects the overall heat buffering of the structure, especially compared to a wholly stone structure.

Why did we go for the timber-framed option for the upper half of the walls? Two factors came into play. One was the increasing difficulty of

Fitting hazel rods into
the timber-framed
upper walls in
September 2003.

building the flint wall above two metres. We were already operating off
low scaffolds and the physical effort of lifting the materials up was slowing
the rate of work down. Scaffolds could have been made higher and we
know the Romans could build flintwork above two metres but there was
a real physical constraint. The other factor is that it has been frequently
suggested that many Roman buildings were part timber-framed and we
felt that we should wrestle with the problems associated with this type of
structure. We know that the Romans seem to have introduced the practice
of timber-framing to this country presumably as part of the methods of
the Roman army. It also seems that completely timber-framed buildings
became more common again in late and post-Roman building traditions.
We have gone for a sort of halfway house solution. This would not have
been approved of by Vitruvius, but he was writing of an urban context:

> As for half-timbered walls, I for one wish they had never been
> invented. However advantageous they are in terms of speed
> and for covering broad expanses, they are still a greater source
> of disaster, and on a large scale, because they are as good as
> torches when it comes to catching fire . . . Even the half timbers

56

*used in plasterwork create fissures because of the placement of
their uprights and cross-pieces.*[5]

MEET THE FLINT STONES . . .

As we have seen, the lower two metres were built out of flint and lime
mortar. The Roman acquisition of flint would have been easy as flint
nodules still lie all over the fields, turned up by cultivation. Picking up
flints and bringing them back to the building site would just have been
a very time-consuming and unskilled occupation. We must also
consider the fact that not all flints are of the same size and that the
wall-building technique needs long ones to tie back into the body of
the wall as well as short ones. So we might reasonably assume that a
degree of sizing of the flints would have taken place on site in preparation for building – but I must admit that this is just an assumption
based on no evidence whatsoever. While some flints for the Butser

Building the new
hypocaust with
materials including
flints and lime mortar,
August 2002.

Roman villa were picked up from the surrounding fields the majority
of the material came from sea-dredged sources that needed to be
picked over to select the flints. It is fair to say that this phase of
bringing the material actually on the site took up about twenty per
cent of the building time. And while we are on figures approximately
two hundred tons of flint were used in building the walls to their
present height. So, while the collection and sorting of flints was time-
consuming but simple for the Romans, the preparation of the lime
mortar was, and is, rather more complicated.

## . . . AND THE LIMESTONES

To make lime mortar you first have to begin with limestone or chalk –
so if you are in an area without these rocks – tough – you'll either have
to carry the lime or use something else, which is why dry-stone building,
timber construction or the use of mud in various forms is not just a

whim. The limestone then has to be heated to around one thousand degrees centigrade and during this process it releases its carbon dioxide. Then it is called quicklime. To turn it into 'slaked' lime it is wetted with water. This hydrates the quicklime which decomposes, giving off a strong heat and spitting with the chemical reaction (it is quite a dangerous process), and forms a putty-like material. This putty is then mixed with materials such as sand to make the lime mortar. To give you some idea of quantities, about twenty tons of quicklime were needed for the walls and about seven tons for the plastering and rendering.

In Roman times the limestone could be processed in two ways – in a kiln with a fire at the bottom, or burned in the open air. One problem with the open air method is that if it rains part-way through the process the burned limestone may be prematurely slaked. Also the fuel for burning needs to generate as intense heat a possible, so it needs to be dry. The Roman writer Cato writes about constructing lime-kilns in his *De Fornace Calcaria*. He describes the dimensions of the kiln and the need to be able

Lime is sieved prior to wetting and turning into lime mortar, May 2003.

to clear the stokehole of ash. He warns to guard it against the wind and when it is lit to 'be careful not to neglect it at night or at any other time' and 'This shall be the sign when the lime is calcinated [turned into quicklime]: the stones at the top should be burnt, the calcinated stones at the bottom will settle and a less smoky flame will come out.' The lime burner can then sell the quicklime to the user as it is easier (and lighter) to transport than the stones, which need to be kept dry. As an alternative the lime burner can slake the lime and store the putty in pits covered with earth and then sell it. Covered slaked lime can stay plastic for a long time – Pliny says that the builders of Rome were advised to only use slaked lime after it had been in store for three years. This isn't quite as daft as it sounds. The chemical reaction with slaking the quicklime can go on for some time. If you use newly slaked lime it can still be 'working', which is not too bad if you are using it for mortar in the walls, but isn't very good if you use it for plaster as, if the chemical reaction is still going on, it will cause 'blisters' or bubbles. So for wall plaster you really need matured lime putty, which is more expensive.

So we have the slaked lime or lime putty. This can easily be turned into lime-wash to act as a paint by diluting it with seventy to eighty per cent water by weight. To make the stuff that glues stones together – mortar – it needs to be mixed with various substances called aggregates. For building mortar these are usually sand – for flooring material such as *opus signinum* they will be other materials like brick fragments or brick dust. In Roman times the sand and water were mixed with the slaked lime in pitsn near the building site, preferably in a sheltered place. The water is added a little at a time to the heap of lime and sand than a tool rather like a right-angled hoe was used to stir the mixture together and to break up the lumps. Once the mixture is ready it will stay plastic for some time. For the mortar in the walls a mixture of one lime to five sand was used.

## MORTAR BORED

The building technique for the wall depends upon the use of flint. Flint is knobbly and irregularly shaped. So lime mortar is needed to fill in the gaps and holes between the flints and to bond them together to stop them falling apart from each other. A layer of mortar is trowelled onto the wall surface (wearing gloves so as to avoid 'lime-burn'), the flints are then laid into it and pushed or hammered so they bind in and make contact in part with the flints below. Long flints are used across the wall to help bond or 'lock' the structure together. In bulk there is more stone than mortar and unlike a brick wall where the bricks are

# A Dash of Lime ... by Ian Pritchett I. J. P. Building Conservation Limited

**dispatches from the front line**

**BACK** in 1994 I had a phone call from Peter Reynolds. He was looking to buy some lime to build a Roman villa. However his budget for the whole project didn't even cover the cost of the lime putty!

This proved to be quite fortunate because it provoked a meeting and discussion. I suggested that Roman builders wouldn't have used lime putty for making mortar. They would have used a hot mix of quicklime, sand and water. And, since it was cheaper this way, it was agreed. So started one of the largest hot mortar projects of recent times. I got to know Peter well as the Villa progressed (slowly in the early days). When Peter died, I thought the project might die with him, but I was delighted to see it continue as it has. It was a great pleasure to watch the progress and help, where I could, throughout the good and bad times. The lime-mortared flint walls suffered because they were still wet over the winter, but recovered brilliantly when the weather warmed up again.

I particularly enjoyed being able to design and help build the timber framed upper storey and roof. This was a compromise between creating our interpretation of what a Roman roof would have looked like and achieving a structure of the necessary size, within the time and budget. I have been stunned by the fantastic results obtained by the whole team on this project.

separated by mortar it must be emphasised that the flints do have some physical contact with each other. This is different from some other more modern flint walls where the flints are laid in level courses and used almost like bricks. The rate of build, once things have been sorted out and in the right weather conditions for lime-mortar the build rate could reach one cubic metre per person, per day. But this

The walls at full height, July 2003. They are built entirely of flints and lime mortar like the Sparsholt villa and do not use layers of tile like other Roman buildings.

was only after having the lime slaked and ready for use and the flints sorted and within easy reach – as has already been said you need to add another twenty per cent of time to allow for this.

One aspect of the flint walls of Butser Roman villa that has caused comment is the absence of tile 'bonding' or levelling courses as part of the build. This is a Roman technique where on top of a layer of flint one or more layers of tile are laid to give a level surface onto which more layers of flint can be added. The Butser Roman villa does not have this. Why not? One reason is that this did not seem to be the technique used at the Sparsholt villa. This notion cannot be based on the surviving walls, as they do not stand very high but is indicated by the amount of tile surviving on site. Sparsholt is not unique in this aspect and there are other Roman sites with walls which do not show this technique. The archaeological evidence is mixed. Another reason is that it was felt that the presence of such a layer would cause a line, or lines, of weakness in the walls and would not provide any bonding above what the flint provided. The Meonstoke collapsed façade seems to have 'broken' on such lines. Sometimes tile seems to have been used merely for a decorative effect and it is interesting to note that certainly some tile is only 'skin deep'. But if you are planning to plaster the outside of the villa and to paint it, why go for an effect which will be hidden? So while we could have used tile bonding/levelling courses, we didn't. We are, however, planning to build some of the retaining walls around the villa, which will stand to about one and a half metres high, with tile courses in order to see what happens. Lastly, we did put in a levelling course on top of the walls to take the base of the timber frame. This was done largely in the form of terracotta known as 'brick' but could equally well have been done all in tile.

One of the problems of working with lime mortar is that due to its high water content and slower drying time, unlike modern concrete, it cannot be used throughout the year. The problem is not so much about the effect of frost, although this does come into it, but that the mortar remains 'plastic' and malleable for much longer. So with the arrival of autumn the lack of warmth in the sun, the absence of warm drying winds, and an increased likelihood of rain all increase the time the lime mortar takes to 'set'. The practical effect of this is that when you try to build on top of one layer and 'beat' the stones into new mortar, the mortar below, not having hardened enough, bulges out, and the wall gets a curve. This can also happen more slowly through the

During the winter of 2002–3 the site had to be covered with a marquee to protect the still malleable lime mortar.

weight of flint and mortar on the layers below. Making it is physically impossible to carry on building. I have described in Chapter 3 the added problems we had with the weather in the autumn of 2002 and we had stopped building completely by Christmas. The need then was to protect the wall tops as built from rain penetration and also to try to minimise the effect of frost; therefore, the wall tops were covered in a layer of straw. This was not thatched, as was traditional ancient practice, but made up into long sausages covered in plastic sheeting, which was easier to do and had the same effect. Part of the villa continued to be covered with the marquee to protect it from the worst of the weather but even there the wall tops were covered with straw against the frost. Some work continued over the winter months and, in

March, when we started building at full strength again the walls had stabilised so there was no more 'bulging'. The mortar had dried enough for work to continue without threatening the stability of the fabric. There was some frost damage – not in the main fabric of the walls but mostly on the surfaces. This took the effect of a 'bloom' of lime mortar which had been affected by the frost crystals. This was easily enough dealt with by using a coarse brush to take this surface off; the good thing with lime mortar was that this could be used again. There was more serious damage to the chalk blocks which had been used to turn the corners of doorways. These had not been adequately covered they had, in cases, split under the influence of the frost and had to be replaced. Otherwise the structure had come through the winter well and formed the basis on which we could proceed in the spring of 2003.

It is interesting to consider comparative figures for other Roman building projects. The construction in the third century of the Saxon shore forts involved a great deal of material and manpower. It has been assumed that the construction of these forts was carried out by a compulsory levy of the civilian population. The proportion of skilled against unskilled workforce was estimated at about six per cent skilled to ninety-four per cent unskilled. The skilled workforce would be people such as carpenters and masons. Calculations made for the construction of Pevensey Castle, West Sussex – with walls made of flint in mortar – suggested that three and a third man days were needed per cubic metre of wall. This compares with a figure of say one and a half man (and woman) days for Butser. Another assumption is that building work is carried out between March or April and November in any one year, making a

Mixing up daub using
earth and straw,
August 2003.

building season length of around two hundred and eighty days which we found makes good sense given a dryish autumn. We will revisit the question of Roman build rates in later chapters.

## WATTLING AND DAUBING

The upper parts of the walls are timber-framed. We will come on to a

discussion of timber sources and sizes in Chapter 6 when we look at the roof, but what interests me now is the question of how the timber framing was filled in. We built a frame about one metre high on top of the walls. Naturally, we needed to fill this in to make it wind- and water-tight. This could be done with a variety of materials – flints or tiles could be mortared in between the timbers; the mud bricks or cob discussed previously could also serve a purpose; planks could be nailed across the outside of the timbers to give a form of cladding, and if this was done on both sides insulating material, such as wool, could be packed in between. All these suggestions are feasible and there is archaeological evidence for some of them. But the technique that we decided to use is of wattle and daub panels which have the advantage of using locally resourced materials and being a likely

Hazel rods are woven into wattle in situ, August 2003.

technique that the Romans would have used. Hazel rods are cut and woven into a lattice *in situ*. They are then coated in daub, which is a mixture of earth or clay and chalk with straw or grass. When this has dried it can then be plastered with the usual lime plaster and then painted if desired. There are a variety of ways the wattle panels can be woven. The 'normal' way is for uprights to be inserted in the panels and then for the thinner rods to be woven horizontally. However, there is a recognised

Roman technique where larger flat battens are set horizontally and the wattle is then woven vertically. It has been suggested that this method allows for prefabricated wattle panels to be inserted in slots running down the upright timbers. While we have not gone in for prefabrication of these panels we have used both techniques to weave the wattle *in situ*.

There were sixty four panels measuring one metre by one and a half metres. One person could weave one and a half panels in a day.

Daub is applied thickly to fill out the gaps in the wattle, August 2003.

## WHEN I'M BUILDING WINDOWS . . .

One of the problems that we had in building the walls was deciding where the windows should go in the rooms, how they would look from the outside and inside, and the heights and dimensions which should be involved. This is a problem because so few Roman buildings survive above floor level, so that even if we find the remains of a collapsed window we cannot be certain exactly how it fitted into the fabric. Based on all the categories of evidence there are two shapes of windows involved. These are the round-headed ones which seem to be very 'classical' and Roman, and then there are the square ones.

Round-headed windows occur in a number of contexts and are well known on Roman sites around the Mediterranean. They are also found both in existing Roman façades and in representations of Roman villas on wall-paintings in Trier, Germany. Nearer Butser in Hampshire we have the example of the actual round-headed windows surviving from the aisled building façade at Meonstoke. So we can be fairly certain that round-headed windows are in the architectural vocabulary for the Butser Roman villa. Square or rectangular windows are rather more difficult. Because round-headed windows have to have their heads turned in brick, tile or masonry they survive in existing fabric and leave indications even when the windows collapse. Square windows are easily made out of wood, with wooden frames. These can be inserted in stone walls. When the building collapses the wood rots and the rubble surround can disintegrate without any trace of the former opening surviving. But we do have some clues to help us: the stone 'models' which we are using to guide us in the appearance of our villa show square windows. It also makes sense to have square rather than round-headed windows if the basic fabric of the building, in whole or part, is timber-framed. Ever tried to put a round-headed window in a square timber frame? Lastly, as we shall see, the metal window grilles that survive from Roman villas are square – so we can be sure that there were square windows. How many and exactly where is still the problem.

The limited evidence that we have of the heights of windows in the façade of a building seems to indicate that they were set with the sill standing at around one and a quarter metres from ground level. This evidence comes mostly from bathhouses so it might be suspect but it is the best we have. A window from a Roman town house at Dorchester had a sill only around seventy-six centimetres above ground level rising to an existing height of around one and a quarter metres.

PLASTER MASTERS

It has already been mentioned that for plastering you need a well-matured lime putty. The first stage is the 'dubbing out' of the walls. This means taking a fairly coarse mix of lime putty and sand and starting the process of smoothing out the worst irregularities. This is especially true of a flint wall. This application is then kept rough and before it has dried what is really the first coat of wall plaster is applied. The tools that were used would be recognisable to modern plasterers and included trowels and the flat boards known as 'floats'. When this layer has been applied it is then 'scored' (that is, the surface is cut) in a variety of ways to provide a key for the next layer. At times this scoring, which can be in diagonal, diamond or wavy combed patterns, has been given a greater significance by archaeologists but it is nothing but an age-old plastering technique. The plaster can then be built up layer by layer. If the wall is to be painted there may be several layers and the last layer will be used for *fresco* painting. The evidence from most Romano-British sites is that usually only a couple of layers of plaster were applied. Achieving a perfect finish was not high on the agenda. However, the mix used for wall plaster was usually finer than that for mortar to give a smoother surface. This is achieved by increasing the proportion of lime to sand in the mix – so instead of one part slaked lime to five parts sand for wall mortar it moves to one part lime putty to three parts sand. While most of the time the plaster was used without the addition of binding agents there is evidence for the limited use of hair and rather more for the use of hay.

Plaster is applied to provide a smooth surface to the walls, July 2003.

For providing a foundation for plastering ceilings you need something which is light but will also be suitable for forming a good bond with the plaster. We know from the literature and from surviving plaster that reed tied together in bundles and attached to the ceiling was used to give this base. Reed can also be used to give a basis for plastering timber partitions where there is no wattle and daub or other such material to provide this.

So, having build up the walls using flints, lime mortar, wattle and daub, and having smoothed them with plaster, lets warm things up a bit and see how the Romans heated their homes ...

Steve Terrell builds the round-headed windows, May 2003.

Testing the hypocaust central heating system, May 2003.

# 5 TURNING UP THE HEAT

One of the great civilising changes that the Romans are popularly supposed to have brought to Britain are heated rooms and heated bathhouses. The Roman historian Tacitus, referring to the activities of Agricola, the Roman governor of Britain around AD 80, says: 'to induce a people . . . uncivilised and therefore prone to fight, to grow pleasurably inured to peace and ease . . . And so the Britons were gradually led on to the amenities that make vice agreeable – baths and sumptuous banquets.'[1] And an important aspect of these activities was heating. We will be looking at the question of underfloor heating in this chapter, but there is a lot more to heating Roman villas than that and I hope that it will not have escaped your attention that of the eight rooms in the Butser villa only one has underfloor heating and in our building there is no bathhouse.

## HEAT LIKE THE ROMANS HEAT . . .

If we look at the reconstructed Iron Age houses at Butser, and better still if we experience them when there is a fire lit, in the centre, we can see that once the fire gets going the smoke rises and, without the aid of chimneys or vents, escapes (leaks is a better word) through small gaps in the thatch. So to heat a space you do not need to have a fireplace against a wall or a ventilator in the roof. The layer of smoke hanging in the house just above your head also acts as a good preservation agent, especially for foodstuffs – ever heard of smoked ham? Long after the Romans left Britain this sort of central fire recurs in high-status medieval dwellings and the great hall of Henry VIII at Hampton Court started off with one. So why did the Romano-British abandon the practice?

Part of the answer is presumably a wish to be adopting Roman standards or demonstrating Roman 'attitude'. It is a mark of 'civilisation' to heat in a Roman rather than a 'native' manner. If you are a 'dedicated follower of fashion' then a hypocaust and dining room with mosaics and painted wall plaster are *de rigueur*. The Roman site at Whitton in South Glamorgan (not far from the villa at Llantwit Major) offers a good example. The excavator, Professor Michael Jarrett, categorised the site as a 'prosperous romanized farm, rather than as the mansion of a wealthy family'.[2] It appears to have had no bathhouse, and no mosaics or traces of mosaics were found although the presence of coloured glass vessels and wall plaster indicate some pretensions to Roman lifestyles, and the iron *styli* indicate some degree of literacy. However, in two areas of the site, traces were found of hypocaust rooms that had been started but apparently never

Uncovering the hypocaust at Sparsholt in 1970.

finished or fired. There is something of a mystery about these rooms as *pilae* (the pillars which heat up and hold up the floor in some types of hypocaust) and wall plaster were found in the debris, indicating the presence of some higher status features on site. Unfortunately, the site had been badly damaged by ploughing, so much of the evidence had gone or been disturbed. We do not know why these rooms were started but never finished (lack of money, death of family, amalgamation with another estate?) but the start made on hypocausts shows the emphasis put on them as status features. Whitton trembles on the edge of becoming a 'villa' but, I feel, doesn't quite make it although Professor Jarrett says 'doubtless, the Romans called it villa'.[3]

Another factor that we should consider in thinking about heating needs in Roman Britain is the question of climate and temperature. We derive this information from the records of the time, which naturally tend to record the exceptional or 'disastrous' such as great snowfalls or frosts which were severe enough to freeze rivers. For example, there were great snowfalls in AD 125, 242, 329 and 341. Other indications of

*Pilae* made with round tiles called *imbrices* from the hypocaust at Rockbourne Roman villa.

the climate can be found from peat formation and lake sediments, and while tree ring width changes can sometimes be used they are not very reliable for our period. Based on a combination of the available evidence it seems that while the later part of the Iron Age was cooler and wetter than present conditions, the Roman occupation of Britain coincided with a period where the climate, which was similar to today's to begin with, became warmer by around one degree centigrade in the third and fourth centuries and dryer than modern times. Later it became very cold, and it seems that around AD 400 there was rapid cooling in the climate with colder winters and cooler summers. This perhaps accounts for one of the letters of Sidonius Apollinaris in AD 484 when he apologises for the delay in transcribing and editing some of his earlier letters:

> *I did not allow the wintry season to interfere with my resolve of fulfilling your desire, though the copyist was hindered by the cold which prevented the ink drying on the page; the drops froze harder than the pen, and as the hand pressed the point on the page they seemed to break from it rather than flow.*[4]

Remains of the bathhouse at Welwyn Roman villa.

While there may be some literary embellishment, it does make the point that colder conditions than those we would find acceptable today could have prevailed in Roman houses especially if they had been designed for warmer times. The ink would probably have been made from some dark substance such as soot and mixed with water, so we are really dealing with the freezing temperature of water. Anybody over the age of forty will remember the cold winter conditions inside British houses which did not have central heating, and the way that greater discomfort was simply accepted.

So, in considering the heating systems for our villa we can assume a slightly warmer climate and a greater acceptance of discomfort from the cold than we would accept. Tied in to this the 'villa' would also show the status of the owner by displaying socially fashionable 'Roman' heating systems.

### . . . DRESS LIKE THE ROMANS DRESS

The first aspect of keeping warm is clothing. What do we know about Roman clothing? It is worth pointing out that they didn't just wear togas. Togas are a big subject but generally speaking they were formal wear, kept 'for best'. Two clues lead us to think that in Britain the Romans could dress warmly. First, they seem to have had several layers of clothing both for males and for females. But the Romans did not really distinguish between outside and inside wear, so cloaks and capes would be regarded as appropriate and respectable indoor clothing. In the later Roman period a form of tights with feet were used to cover the legs and it did seem to become respectable for all classes to adopt the slave- or labouring-class habit of wearing tunics unbelted. It is also interesting to note that one of the fashion exports of Roman Britain in the early fourth century is a woollen hooded cloak called the *Byrrus Britannicus*. At the same time the changing fashion in men's hairstyles from crew cut and short beard to clean-shaven and combed forward locks seems to be more to do with a looking to past 'golden ages' and the official adoption of Christianity than any climatic trends to. The last pagan Roman Emperor, Julian, not only defiantly wore a beard but also wrote a treatise 'against the beard-haters'.

The Emperor Julian complete with beard.

## HYPOCAUSTS

Hypocausts are a way of heating rooms by circulating heat, usually generated from an external fire or furnace, under a floor and venting it

Diagram showing the
construction and
passage of fumes
through the Butser
hypocaust.

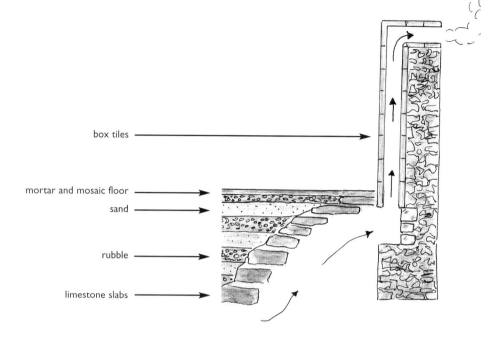

box tiles

mortar and mosaic floor

sand

rubble

limestone slabs

via flues up through the walls. This system means that the floor becomes hot or warm and so do the walls. Hypocausts are most associated with Roman bathhouses, these had several rooms that diminished in temperature the further they were from the heat source. The final moment of the bathing cycle was a bracing cold water plunge. In this bathhouse system the need was for swift and efficient circulation of the hot air so the tendency was to carry the floor above the hot air circulation area on the smallest pillars (known as *pilae*) possible. This would maximise the hot air circulation area and if the *pilae* were rounded they would hinder the circulation less. This sort of bathhouse hypocaust had an increased fire risk and this is one of the reasons why bathhouses are sometimes located away from the main complex. Bathhouse hypocausts also occur in some villas, including at Sparsholt where the aisled building had been adapted to incorporate a small bathhouse.

Domestic bathhouses were not always kept fired up and ready to use. The amount of fuel that they consumed and the labour involved in producing it must have been significant. This problem occurred widely, and Pliny made sure that his favourite villa was close to public baths in case his own were not working. Sidonius not only recognises the problem but offers a solution on how to have a 'Roman bath' when the bathhouse is not ready. He is travelling close to two sets of friends, both with villas:

> *Both of our hosts had baths in their houses, but in neither did they happen to be available; so I set my own servants to work in the rare sober interludes which the convivial bowl, too often filled, allowed their sodden brains. I made them dig a pit at their best speed either near a spring or by the river; into this a heap of red-hot stones was thrown, and the glowing cavity then covered over with an arched roof of wattled hazel. This still left interstices, and to exclude the light and keep in the steam given off when water was thrown on the hot stones, we laid coverings of Cicilian goats' hair over all. In these vapour-baths we passed*

Demolishing the original Butser hypocaust in July 2002. Note the rising terracotta vents.

*whole hours with lively talk and repartee; all the time the cloud of hissing steam enveloping us induced a healthy perspiration.*[5]

Having enjoyed this early example of a sauna, they go on to bathe in hot water and, to get rid of their languid feeling, finish off '*with a bracing douche from fountain, well or river'.*

The Butser Roman Villa's hypocaust is of a different type to those found in bathhouses, but the principle of hot air circulating under the floors and up through the walls remains the same. Our hypocaust consists of large blocks of built masonry supporting the floor with hot air channels radiating through the area and then venting out up through flues in the walls. Because of the pattern of channels in this

## Me and My Villa . . .    by Steve Terrell foreman

**FROM** the first days of flint laying to the frantic final days at the end of the project, building the hypocaust is what most sticks in my memory.

I had been working at Butser Ancient Farm at weekends as a volunteer, which is how I met Rick Wilgoss, the Project Manager. At this stage I did not know what a hypocaust was, I just practised flint laying and 'knocking up' lime mortar by hand. Rick asked me what I did for a living and I explained I was a former 'spread' (plasterer). Rick then asked if I could render flint work. I replied that I could, but that it would not be easy. Rick said that if I wanted the job, I would have to build the rest of the villa first!

Rick went on to explain about the project and how he was putting together a team with no preconceived ideas about Roman building. I was loaned a book about Roman building techniques and invited to a dig site to view and study a Roman-built flint wall.

I had a few quiet chats with Butser's celtic farmer, Dave Kirby, a former seafarer like myself, who had worked on the original hypocaust with Peter Reynolds and who told me something of the nature of the man and what he stood for. They were the original build team.

I think one of the hardest decisions made in those early days, was to de-construct Peter's hypocaust and bench it further into the hillside. It was a heartbreaking time to effectively destroy someone's else's work. It was rather quiet around the site until the new hypocaust was well under way. Valuable lessons were learned to assist with rebuilding it, and this was when I started to realise what experimental archaeology was all about.

type of hypocaust they are sometimes known as 'Union Jack' hypocausts. The extensive and rapid circulation of the hot air is not the priority. If it was the floor would just have a few 'hot-spots'. It seems a reasonable possibility that this sort of hypocaust was intended as a sort of 'night storage' heater. In this theory the fire need not be as great as with the other sort of hypocaust, thus saving on fuel, and the intention could be to build up the heat in the masonry blocks over a period so that they give off a more gentle, radiant heat. This would also extend to the walls. We cannot be sure of this but once the hypocaust and floor above have dried out fully we intend to run experiments to see if the theory works and determine the amounts of fuel that would be used. If we are right then this form of radiant heat would seem to be appropriate for a use of the room as a bedroom or a winter dining room. In the Butser Roman villa we have delib- erately increased the potential warmth of the room by making it the only room to have glazed windows which do not open, and by having a low ceiling which means less heat lost to the roof. We know from the literature that in some cases the Romans accepted and made use

Building up the walls of the hypocaust in August 2002. Note the arched entrance for stoking the fire and the box tiles rising up through the wall.

of the fact that the heating of one room affected the adjoining ones. In our case it will be interesting to see how the temperature of the larger room adjoining the hypocaust room will be affected and also the areas over the ceilings, which have storage or even sleeping potential.

So how did the hot, or warm, air and fumes pass through the walls and exit the building? It is generally accepted from surviving archaeo- logical evidence that the first stage of transferring the heat, smoke and fumes from under the floor was usually by means of square or rectan- gular sectioned tile pipes known as 'box tiles'. In Latin they are known as a *tubulus*. While we tend to think of Roman inventions as having always been around, the Roman philosopher called Seneca (who was driven to suicide by the Emperor Nero in AD 65) said that box tiles were amongst the inventions of his life time. British box tiles have a wide variety of size and shape. The height ranges from around four hundred and fifty down to one hundred and fifty-five millimetres, width from three hundred and thirty to one hundred and thirty millimetres and depth from two hundred and eighty to eighty-five millimetres. Laid in the wall they form an efficient fireproof flue.

In ancient Roman sites box-tile flues are found in the walls clearly leading up from underfloor spaces, but we then have a problem knowing what happens to them because we have very few high-standing Roman walls with box-tile flues in them and there is no evidence as to how box-tile flues exited the buildings. If the walls were all of masonry and there was a tile or stone roof it is feasible to think that the box tiles could have continued up through the walls and exited in some fashion out of the roof. We might think that, although the heat in the flues would be quite low, it would be sensible not to have contact between the flues and the wood of the roof. However, that idea might just reflect modern health and safety concerns, and maybe the Romans would not have been bothered? But the problem becomes more urgent if we are dealing with a half-timbered building. In many cases this would mean that box-tile flues would be in direct contact with the horizontal timbers of the roof structure and with wattle and daub panels. While building the Butser villa, we quickly concluded that another approach must be experimented with.

We took clues from two sources. Firstly, while most Roman box tiles are complete with holes at either end, a number have holes of varying sizes cut in the side. These holes are not cut after firing; they are made when the clay is wet. In other words these 'side-vented' box tiles are designed in this way, meaning that the heat and fumes are meant to be able to travel both ways. The second clue lies in the way that the flues exit from the bathhouse at Herculaneum. Here the vertical flues open out into horizontal tunnels in the masonry between the top of the vaults and the flat roof and from there via window-like openings into the open air. Taking these two together we have constructed the flues so that the vertical sections exit near the tops of the walls and that, for the interior walls, the flues are joined together by a horizontal run of box tiles to a common exit on an outside wall. We have tried the system with smoke and we know that it works. This approach explains the lack of chimneys on representations of villas, it also reduces the fire risk and seems to fit the archaeological evidence. Is it right? Well, we can't be one hundred per cent sure and just in case we are wrong we have left it so that the vertical flues can, with some simple unblocking, be vented out of the top of the walls, however that might be. For the moment we await the further trials on it and the reactions of the archaeological community.

## FIREPLACES

One different feature about the Sparsholt villa on which the ground floor plan of the Butser Roman villa was based was the presence in Room Seven of a 'fireplace'. The evidence for this was the presence of a recess in the wall lined with tiles and with a hearth or apron in front and tile 'cheeks' to either side. There was evidence of burning around this area. Like the rest of the Sparsholt villa this feature did not rise very high so we had no way of knowing how it continued

Smoke rises in the flues from beneath the floor to window height before exiting the building horizontally, May 2003.

up the wall and, if there was an aperture, how it exited to the outside world. This feature was not unique to Sparsholt. Comparable features have been identified by the archaeologist David Johnston all over central southern England with a concentration in what is now Hampshire (including ten in Silchester) and the Isle of Wight and outliers as far as Somerset and the Roman town of Verulamium. Inevitably they vary in detail and we need to remember that while they all generally look alike they may not all have the same function If we put this to one side we still have two problems. One is to try

A Roman skillet made of bronze from Faversham in Kent. Like the 'fireplace' it may well have had a ceremonial rather than culinary function.

and work out what most of them are and the second is how to construct the Butser Roman villa example based on the best evidence available.

So what are they? In order to answer this question we need to know what they look like. The most complete example comes from the Star villa at Shipham in Somerset which does seem to show that they are formed by having some sort of canopy coming out over the apron area. This suggestion seems to be borne out by evidence from the way that the mortar traces on the collapsed tiles found at

The unfinished 'fireplace' at Butser Roman villa, May 2003.

Charcoal brazier like the Romans used to heat their rooms.

Sparsholt showed that part of them were exposed and not stuck to another tile. This seems to indicate that the tiles were cantilevered into the room. But while we assume that there is a vent rising up from the feature we cannot be sure. There is certainly no blocking above the gap on any of our surviving examples. However, there is a well-known archaeological saying, 'absence of evidence is not evidence of absence', so we need to be cautious. Then what could the feature be? One possibility is that it might have been a recess for a shrine. I am afraid that there is another archaeological saying which is 'in case of doubt call it ritual'. This is on the grounds that if no reasonable explanation can be found for a feature, all that remains is religion. The evidence that our feature was involved in burning would not contradict its use as a shrine where offerings could be burned. However, the positioning on the ground, the presence of a 'hood', the apron in front and the large amounts of burning and associated food debris in some cases all suggest that we are dealing with a fireplace or hearth. There is a difference between the two. It could be a low-level hearth normally with a brazier set on it charged either by charcoal, wood or coal. In this case it would be useful to have a flue to vent smoke and fumes out of the room. The fumes would be especially relevant in the case of the charcoal-fired brazier. This would be used for cooking or heating. Alternatively, it might be a proper fireplace with a fire set at the back and a vent to act as a proper chimney. Did the Romans have chimney pots? There is a type of artefact which some have called a chimney pot. It consists of a clay cylinder-like object with decorative slots cut in the side. The problem with these is that there is no clear proof that these were ever used as chimneys and I think that it is more probable that they were perhaps ventilators of some sort or, more likely, decorative roof finials.

And of course, if you want to vent out you could follow the practice seen around the Mediterranean and have a flue coming up to the roof line, in stone or box tile and simply cover it from the elements by two flat tiles to form an inverted 'v' or triangle. This would be very difficult to identify archaeologically from the collapse of a roof. In Butser we have constructed the feature without a vent but may make one from box tiles later on, and take it out through the roof.

We have some literary evidence of fireplaces in action in the Roman world. They do not give the picture of clean and efficient Roman living that we might expect. Describing his villa at Aviaticum Sidonius writes:

> *The winter dining room is entered from this corridor; a roaring fire on an arched hearth often fills this apartment with smoke and smuts. But that detail I may spare you; a glowing hearth is the last thing I am inviting you to enjoy just now.*[6]

Or writing to a friend:

> *When your granaries and stores are full you may decide to pass the snowy months of Janus and Numa in rural ease by your smoking hearth until swallow and stork reappear.*[7]

85

So the Romans are used to fires and they recognise that they do not always draw well. How did they heat rooms if they did not have hypocausts or hearths and did not just want to wrap up warmly? The answer seems to have been by portable braziers using charcoal. Because they are portable we do not easily find them and the Romans appear to have been careful not to allow them to burn the floors, although at the Sparsholt villa there was scorching of the reception room mosaic floor, presumably caused by a brazier. The braziers are rather like a modern barbecue. The trays seem to be enclosed so hot embers or ashes do not drop on the floor. The main source of scorching could be from the legs and presumably these could be rested on tiles. I am making a number of assumptions here because we have not yet tested our Roman braziers properly to to see if the legs become very hot. This is one of the experiments we would be hoping to do in the future. The other problem with this type of charcoal-burning braziers is the production of lethal gases. In those rooms which are open to the structure this space, allied with the draughty nature of the villa (see the sections about windows and doors), this was probably not a problem. In rooms with ceilings it could well cause difficulties. Again this is something we would like to monitor in the completed villa.

Meanwhile, even though we have worked out how to keep warm in our villa we still haven't talked about keeping dry: our villa needs a roof . . .

Cooking on charcoal in the kitchen, October 2003.

The villa in August 2003. The roof frame has been erected and boarded over prior to tiling.

# RAISING
# THE ROOF

The raw materials needed to construct a Roman roof are wood, stones or tiles to cover it and iron (especially in the form of nails). But before we can cover the roof we need to build the wooden frame that gives it shape, and remember, we are trying to stick to local materials that would have been available to the Romans. So what can we say about the wood that might have been available to construct our Roman villa in south Hampshire? Well, because we do not have any Roman water-logged deposits in the area, we do not have any examples of Roman wood to help us. We are also short of relevant peat deposits so we cannot even look to this source to indicate what trees might have been available, although one recent study has suggested that southern Roman Britain was more heavily wooded than at present. In the absence of this sort of local evidence we have to look elsewhere for the types of actual wood used and also make some guesses about what was happening in terms of tree types in this area in the Roman period.

## A WALK IN THE WOODS

Faventius, following Vitruvius, writes that oak is the best wood for building, but adds that beech is useful in dry places although it rots in water and says that elm and ash quickly warp in any structure and are not to be favoured. In the beech-growing area of the Chilterns, the late medieval timber-framed buildings are all in oak and it could be that the Romans favoured it in a similar way. As we have some labour values for the daily rate for workmen in the sections on floors and paintings in Chapters 7 and 8 it is worth noting that in AD 301 oak and ash cost 250 denarii for seven yards of timber nine inches square. The daily rate for a skilled craftsman was around fifty denarii and the value of the 'squared' timber must reflect the labour input.

It is worth considering the exploitation of wood resources by the Romans. In the Weald for example, Roman ironworks had a huge demand for fuel. If it is assumed that some sort of coppice system was being practised then the estimated 550 tons of iron produced by six

Tombstone of a Roman carpenter from Priolo in Sicily.

out of the thirty-nine known Roman iron-working sites would have needed 46,000 tons of wood, the product of around 23,000 acres of woodland. This is heavy industry, but on a smaller scale it has been estimated that the baths at Welwyn used about twenty-three hectares of coppice annually (producing five tons of wood per hectare) to keep it going – this amounts to the estimated annual labour of one man. These figures seem to be comparable with those given for the fuel needed for one of the public baths at Pompeii which is estimated as a cart-load of wood a day or about 150 tons a year. These estimates give some idea of the quantity of wood needed as fuel for industry and domestic use, for building, fencing and so on.

The wood used for building in Roman London, where the best and nearest samples are to be found, is invariably oak. A study of a first-century timber-framed building in London showed that the majority of timbers came from young trees aged between about twenty-five and sixty years old and measuring between 150mm and 250mm in diameter. These are thought to have come from managed woodlands worked on a coppice cycle. There must also have been larger trees to provide the plank cladding. These larger trees could have grown as 'standards' – large individual trees in areas of coppice or as hedgerow trees. Very few trees show the straight graining that comes from 'wildwood' trees grown in unmanaged woodland. The implication is that if Roman buildings are timber-framed then there must be managed woodland to provide trees in the various sizes that would be needed.

So, if oak rules in London, how about the area now known as Hampshire? For a start the geology is different: it has lots of chalk, and soils formed from chalk are the predominant feature, although there are important variations. This contrasts with the gravel terraces of the Thames valley. If you look at Hampshire today the impression is of beech

– the famous beech 'hangers' or steep slopes around Gilbert White's Selborne. Beech certainly was in use in the Weald for Roman ironworks. Despite being a large tree it never seems to have been popular as a structural timber in England. And while recently it has been treated as a timber tree this perhaps disguises its use up until about two hundred years ago as a coppice tree for smaller wood, or pollarded for wood pasture, and of course, the 'mast' or nuts for the autumn feeding of pigs.

**dispatches from the front line**

## Teamwork at Butser ... by **Thomas Rattray** build team member

**TWO** of my friends told me that they needed help at Butser Ancient Farm to finish building their Roman villa. As an archaeology graduate with some building experience, this was an opportunity I couldn't miss.

Even though we were under a lot of pressure all the way through the project, the whole team has worked together, dealing with the problems that we faced. The rest of the team and the countless volunteers have taught me a lot about the different aspects of the project and the different skills involved.

Because the villa is an experimental project, we have used many different techniques to construct it. For example, there are different types of plaster, some using goat hair and our own hair to bind the layers together. To finish the walls we used a wet plaster suitable for fresco paintings. I found the process of making frescos very interesting and once the paintings were done the villa began to look more like a home. Being the model for one of the figures in the corridor mural was a great honour and I will remember the whole project with a smile on my face.

There is one further factor that we should consider. The Roman elite were very keen on hunting as a form of recreation. Even the scholastic Pliny went hunting although it might have been felt that he let the side down. In a letter to a friend he wrote:

> *you will think it a good joke ... your old friend has caught three*
> *boar ... I was sitting by the hunting nets with writing materials*
> *by my side instead of hunting spears ... making notes so that*

*even if I came home empty-handed I should at a least have my notebooks filled . . . so next time you hunt yourself follow my example and take your notebooks along with your lunch basket and flask . . . Minerva* [goddess of wisdom] *walks the hills no less than Diana* [goddess of hunting].

There is sufficient evidence from the bones of boar and deer to suggest that woodland creatures were present and the evidence of hunting motifs on mosaics suggests that hunting was not only the theoretical occupation of the elite villas owners, but also actively practised. This suggests that woodland was present, had several functions and just might have been 'preserved' to allow for a good supply of game and sport – rather in the way that grouse-moors or pheasant woods are 'preserved' today.

Cutting the roof timbers, July 2003. The Romans would have used a frame and a two-person saw just like this one.

My conclusion is that it would not have been too difficult to find the timber needed for the roof as we have constructed it at Butser, with timber of all sizes including a few very large pieces.

## CHOP, CHOP

So how was the timber processed into usable wood? According to Pliny, Daedalus invented carpentry. Daedalus was the legendary inventor who designed the wings which caused the first air crash when his son, Icarus, flew too close to the sun. Usually ancient carpentry was a bit less dangerous and surviving tools and representations on tomb-stones show that Roman carpenters had all the equipment needed for measuring, marking and working timber.

To measure it up prior to working they had rulers, dividers and knives which could scribe or mark a line. Timber can also be marked by 'snapping' a chalked line across it which gives a straight line. You will find this technique coming up again with the laying out of wall-paintings in Chapter 8.

The trees would have been felled with axes, then sawn to the desired sizes or into boards by means of putting the tree on a trestle and cutting it with a two-man saw.

Trimming then takes place with thin-bladed double-bevelled axes. The slight ripples left on the 'worked' surface of the timber betray the hand finishing: modern sawn timber is very uniform.

The range of joints used by the Romans can all be made with small saws and chisels. They certainly had drills and gouges as well and there is some evidence of auguring or drilling out material in making some of the joints. But, while this would have saved time and energy, the Romans do not appear to have had the custom or mindset to make the connection and these tools were not widely used.

It is worthwhile defining what we mean by a 'joint'. In carpentry it is understood to be a means of joining together two separate lengths of timber. This can be intended to make them form a longer piece in total (often known as a 'scarf') or to be joined at an angle, often a right

half-lap joint

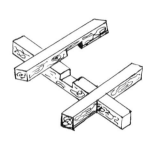

cross-halved joint

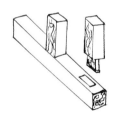

mortice and tenon joint

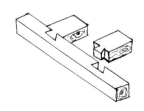

dovetail joint

angle. The choice of joint depends upon the timber as well as the skills available. Joints used by the Romans included the simple 'half-laps' (where the ends of the timber are halved to fit together), and the associated 'cross halving' (to form a right angled joint). The 'mortice and tenon' joint also appears in various forms, where one a piece of the timber has a hole cut in it (the mortice) and the other piece has an extension (the tenon) and the two are then joined. 'Dove-tailed' joints are also used where the cuts are at an angle in the timbers which increases the natural strength of the joint by locking the two together.

What is remarkable is the roughness of much Roman carpentry. The work is not precise so joints would have been lose. Wooden pegs are not used to fix joints – this is probably connected with the limited use of the augur – but nails are widely used. As we will see, with the Romans, it is nails, nails and more nails, and we need to consider what this tells us about Roman building carpentry – not the fine joinery of furniture – but the sort of construction work we are concerned with.

### RAISING THE RAFTERS

Leaving aside those roofs for bathhouses or temples which could be made out of masonry or brick vaults, we start with the basic question:

'what do we know about Roman roofs?', not just the outside appearance but, more importantly, the basic structure which gives the external shape.

If we start with the western Roman Empire, the last ancient building which preserved its roof timbers, St Paul's Outside the Walls, Rome, built between AD 384 and 403 was destroyed by fire in 1823. Otherwise, nothing survives which is of any great help and you probably won't be surprised to learn that there are no timber Roman roofs surviving in Britain. But as we have seen in the chapter on walls, remains from Roman timber buildings survive in the damp conditions alongside the Thames. In these cases it is the absence of evidence of really heavy timbers that is suggestive.

One way of making a roof is for the stone structure to be raised to form gable ends and then for timbers to run horizontally from one gable to the other. These are called 'purlins'. Running across these could be rafters and onto these could go boarding or battens which would be horizontal. Onto this structure slates or tiles could be hung (for battens) or placed (for boards). In larger buildings these stone gables could be formed on interior walls with the same result. This is a possible way of roofing the Butser Roman villa, although there would be a long span across the 'service' or 'kitchen' room. This approach would also give an explanation of why the walls are uniformly so thick. But it does require higher masonry walls with the labour and structural problems involved and the pressures of the roof come on the gable walls. This could come with sideways as well as vertical pressure and might be an explanation of why we find collapsed gable ends in the remains of Roman buildings.

Another way of constructing the roof would be to have what are called 'close coupled rafters'. These are simply the 'down' timbers which can have a cross or 'collar' beams to hold them together. This is what is known as an 'A-frame' roof. The tendency for this roof to move sideways can be counteracted by covering it in horizontal boarding. This is a simple roof and the timbers involved could be numerous but fairly light. The strength comes from repetition.

The last approach, which is the one we have broadly followed at the Butser Roman villa, is to have heavier timber supports in the form of 'trusses'. Our approach follows the example of a reconstructed roof from the late first century AD, based on evidence from excavations at Poultry in the City of London. On a larger scale this is like an A-frame but with a central post and bracing to give extra strength and stability to the roof. These trusses are tied together with horizontal purlins, including a ridge and then boarded over. The logic of the construction demands that the boards run up and down rather than horizontally.

At the Butser Roman villa, while there are four main parts of the roof, there are only three trusses as one of the load-bearing sections has been made of smaller timber in the form of a 'stud' wall. In this case the smaller timbers give the same support as the other trusses but at the expense of having so much timber so close together that the area is virtually partitioned off. This feature is being covered by plaster on reed, so you will not be able to see it in the finished building. You will also see that the timber for the trusses onto the main status rooms, including the reception/summer dining room, has been carefully shaped and finished, while the timber of the truss over the service/kitchen area has been left rougher. We have no proof that this is what happened in Roman villas but we wished to make a point about the potential for different approaches to the treatment of rooms depending upon their Roman status.

In the design of the roof of the Butser Roman villa it was noticed that the plan of the villa, based on the one at Sparsholt, seemed to fall into modules which guided us in the spacing of the roof trusses. These seem to be about four and a half metres wide. So one truss lies across the support provided by the wall dividing the winter dining room from the 'library' and another on the wall between that room and the 'reception' room. So three are regularly spaced. We then hit a problem as the next wall offering support lies out of a spacing order. This is the wall between the service/kitchen room and its associated storage room/ante-room. We resolved this problem in practice by putting the next truss in its proper place in the logical order and adding supports to give it extra strength. This might have been a mistake in Roman terms, as it is conceivable that the Romans might have accepted the change in spacing and put the truss on the supporting wall. For this to work it would have needed a proper gable end together with longer purlins, and might not have been as structurally stable.

This brings us to another problem with the roof and that is the question of the half-hipped ends. If you remember the stone models

Boarding the roof of the villa, September 2003. Note the half-hipped ends.

from Luxembourg, which guide us in how the exterior of a corridor villa might have looked, the ends of the roof ended in an inverted V or triangle. This is felt to be a sound classic form. You will also remember that the local planners wanted the Butser Roman villa to look as much like a local Hampshire vernacular building as possible, especially in the way that it fitted into the landscape. We therefore accepted that a half-hip had to be put on to finish both ends of the roof. There is some evidence for Roman hipped roofs, notably that from Scole in Norfolk

An A-frame for the roof about to be lifted into place. Note the rough hand-cut wood, August 2003.

where what seem to be hip rafters were discovered having been reused. The use of a half-hip at either end increases the lateral stability of the roof and also fits in with the way the truss is carried over the service/kitchen room.

So this gives us the basic design of the roof and we can be reasonably satisfied that the sizes and quantities of timber would be available. How about its actual construction? In the case of the Butser Roman villa the roof was prefabricated off site and then brought on lorries and largely put into place with a crane. If we had been actually doing it in Roman times I would have expected the timber to be found locally within, say, a five to ten mile radius of the site. The larger trees could be felled and roughly trimmed to shape to reduce the weight then transported to the site. Teams of oxen could have dragged them or they could have been put on sledges. There is evidence for the prefabrication of roof timbers in Roman times before erection and simple lifting mechanisms like sheer-legs could have lifted the timbers. While it would have been more difficult to lift the main timbers onto the top of a two metre wall than to erect them on low stone foundations, it would not have been impossible, especially given the supply of labour which we think would have been available. So while the erection of the roof in Roman times would have probably taken far longer than the ten days it took us with a crane it could have been done.

Another problem we faced was the finish of the timber. Would all the timber on display have been squared by hand? We have no firm answers but decided that the 'status' timbers for the trusses which would be seen from the main reception/summer dining room and the 'library' next to the hypocaust room would be hand-finished and square because they would be on public display. Many of the other timbers would be left 'in the round' and with the bark on and only trimmed if they were to have structural additions – for example, the purlins had one side flat to take the roofing boards. We accept that this 'rough' treatment would be bound to cause debate. It was also the intention from the start that these timbers, as with the underside of the boarded roof, would be whitewashed and perhaps have some motifs painted on them. As it turned out, in transporting the timber the bark was often damaged, leaving a very messy finish. This, no doubt, would have occurred in Roman times, perhaps to a worse extent. So the decision was taken to strip the bark on some of the timbers and leave the timber still in the round but bare and ready for painting. What we want to try to escape is the stereotypical view of idealised Roman buildings inherited from the Renaissance and Hollywood and try to approach the problem from other angles.

Many of the timbers would be left 'in the round' and with the bark still on as with these purlins which simply have one side flattened to take the boards, August 2003.

One of the points that I found most difficult to take is the crudeness of Roman roof construction. In several cases the ends of the timber was sawn flat, the area to receive it was cut flat with an axe and the joint was formed by simply nailing the one to the other with, say, seven long nails. When discussing it with the roofers I was reassured that although it was crude it would work and the stability of the roof was as great as if the wood had been jointed and pegged. In other cases more elaborate joints have been formed but nails are still used to secure them. I suppose that part of this technique is that it makes it easier to create a roof with less chance of things going wrong – such as joints not fitting or being out of alignment.

So, Roman roofs must not be imagined as one of the glories of the structure and the civilisation with the beautifully carved, pegged joints of medieval church roofs. Roman roofs are utilitarian – beauty and civilisation are expressed in other ways.

It is also surprising to see just how many nails a Roman villa site produces. Nails are the great disposable item of Roman culture. They are used profligately and discarded with no apparent attempt to recycle them. When you consider the labour and resources that had gone into the production of the iron for each nail and then its hand-forging (at say at least two or three minutes per nail) then it represents in total a large effort, but to the Romans nails were dispensable. After the roof frame is erected, boards are simply nailed all over it and it is ready for finishing.

## OUT ON THE TILES

How do we finish the roof? In finding an answer we have two constraints. One is the sort of roofing material found on archaeological excavations – the other is rather more modern and depends on the planning conditions imposed. The planners are concerned about preserving the 'amenity' of the area around Butser which is an Area of Outstanding Natural Beauty and a potential National Park. They want a roof which will 'fit in'. But let's start with the evidence from the archaeology.

The main roof of the Sparsholt Roman villa was covered in grey stone slate made of what is known as Purbeck stone. These are of a shelly limestone quarried on the Isle of Purbeck, Dorset. The slates were cut to a diamond pattern with a flat upper edge. They had one nail hole for securing to the roof. It is thought that they were laid in an overlapping pattern with each new row offset to one side. The distribution of the slates from this area is mostly concentrated in Dorset and Hampshire. The Sparsholt villa was on the edge of the distribution, which presumably gives an idea of the distance these slates could be economically carried. Because of cost, it was not possible to roof the

Ridging the roof, September 2003.

Butser Roman villa in this material so a modern substitute of about the same colour was used and this fitted in with the planning constraints.

We also have to think about how the ridge would be finished. This could be in half-round tiles perhaps with the doubtful chimney pots from Chapter 4 which might really be decorative finials. We do have evidence that on some stone roofs there were specially carved stone ridge pieces.

Alternatively roofs could be covered in terracotta tiles. The 'classic' form of a Roman roof consists of flat tiles with two sides raised (*tegulae,* singular *tegula*) which are laid flat and overlapping each other (like fish scales). The obvious gaps where the flanges butt together are then covered by half-round tiles (*imbrices,* singular *imbrex*). This makes for a relatively watertight roof. It is also possible for the *imbrices* to be used entirely on their own. In this case a line is laid 'upside down' to form a trough and the gap between these lines is covered by another line the other way up. This form is still very common in Mediterranean countries. Another variation observed on Mediterranean tiled roofs is that at between every fourth to sixth row the *tegulae* are inverted over other *tegulae*. This allows the tiler to make corrections of direction and length, especially for roofs which are out of square.

The roof of Butser Roman villa with the tiling almost complete, October 2003.

Fragments of tiles were found at Sparsholt, so while it was decided that on the Butser Roman villa we should initially use grey 'stone' slates, we may later roof the corridor in tiles. This would give a colour difference to two different functions of the building with the corridor being 'read' separately from outside. It would also, we hope, fit in with the vernacular architecture of the area where one roof (usually the main one) can be slate and an extension can be roofed in tile.

The pitch (slope) of the roof also caused some problems. In Britain because we have a reasonable rainfall the pitch of a roof needs to be great

Diamond-shaped overlapping stone tiles coloured with pigments. The Romans used tiles like these on the roofs of some villas.

enough for the water to flow off quickly and not leak in. On the other hand, a steeper pitch needs more wood for the roof and the roofing material must be capable of staying in place, either by its own gravity or by attachment such as nailing or pegging. On the other hand, it must not be so heavy that the roof timbers cannot support it. The pitch will,

Inside the roof during construction, August 2003. The pitch of the main section is thirty-two degrrees and the corridor twenty-five degrees.

therefore, often depend upon the nature of the material roofing the structure. Thatch is a good roofing material but only if it is set at a quite steep angle (say, fifty degrees) to throw the rain down the stalks, and it needs to be firmly bound to the roofing frame. It is also heavy. It should be noted that if a thatched roof were converted to tile, the tiles would need nailing, as they would not stay at that angle under their own weight.

Tiles are set at a lower pitch. In the Mediterranean area this is usually at about twenty to twenty-five degrees. The collapsed gable end from the Redlands Farm villa (Northants) clearly showed a pitch of about twenty-two and a half degrees for a tiled roof. Experiments suggest that on boarded roofs, like the one on the Butser Roman villa, the angle can be increased to about thirty-degrees before slippage becomes a problem. This is with the tiles mortared together but not nailed. Another test has suggested forty degrees as an angle of repose. The penalty of increasing the angle of the pitch is that the number of tiles needed to cover the roof increase. From the number of tiles on a flat roof, a twenty-degree pitch means a six per cent increase, a thirty degree pitch a fifteen per cent increase and a forty-degree pitch a thirty per cent increase. A twenty-five-degree pitch seems in the right order for the corridor to enable uys to tile it later if we choose to.

Stone slates nailed to the boarding can take a steep pitch. We will discuss some of the problems in the next few paragraphs but if thatch needs a fifty-degree slope and tiles a twenty to twenty-five-degree slope then the slope for slates can come in between. The evidence from one roof made out of Purbeck stone roof tiles on the villa at Dewlish, Dorset, suggests a pitch of twenty degrees.

In trying to work out the pitch of the main roof we looked for parallels. The roof of St Paul's outside the Walls, Rome, already referred to, had been surveyed before the fire and had roof pitches of around twenty-five degrees. An obvious British example came from the collapsed façade of the aisled building at Meonstoke in Hampshire. The side aisles of this structure had roof slopes of tile and were estimated to be at about thirty degrees. However, when we come to the main surviving roof the pitch was about forty-seven-and-a-half degrees and the roofing material was sub-hexagonal stone slates. This could be because the building was originally thatched (remember the comment above about the fifty-degree angle of thatched roofs) or because the Romans built them that way. Another collapsed Roman gable end at Carsington, Derbyshire, seems to indicate a roof pitch of forty degrees and, to quote the excavator, 'was unquestionably tiled' at least in part, as stone slates were also found on the site. As more recent examples show, it is possible for a roof to have lower courses in slate and upper ones in tile. The remarks about the relationship to the pitch and number and weight of tiles or slates need to be borne in mind with the structure of these roofs. Both Meonstoke and Carsington were tall buildings and I wonder if the pitch of the roof was meant to increase the impression for the spectator. And then there is the evidence from the Redlands Farm and Dewlish villas for a lower pitch. Such evidence as we have seems to be very contradictory and I can only conclude that we have a lot to learn before we can become more certain. As it is the Butser Roman villa has been built with a lower roof pitch. It is a villa, not an aisled structure, and while we noted the evidence from other sites we preferred to go with the more 'traditional' lower pitches. So around thirty-two degrees for the main roof and twenty-five degrees for the corridor it is!

One last point. On modern houses we have roofing felt directly under the slates or tiles. This provides a waterproof covering in its own right and stops draughts and rain, snow and dirt blowing into the roof space. On earlier (but still not Roman) roofs one way of dealing with this problem was to pack moss between the slates to form a living protective layer or to 'torch' the underside of the slates, that is, to plaster them to stop the cracks. The Romans had no need of this as the boarded roof provided a 'secondary' cover, which, while not quite as good a some other methods – the planks do not join closely – still provides a reasonable way of solving the problem.

So, having put a watertight roof on our villa it is time to go back to ground level and consider Roman flooring, including their famous mosaics . . .

Building the roof, August 2003.

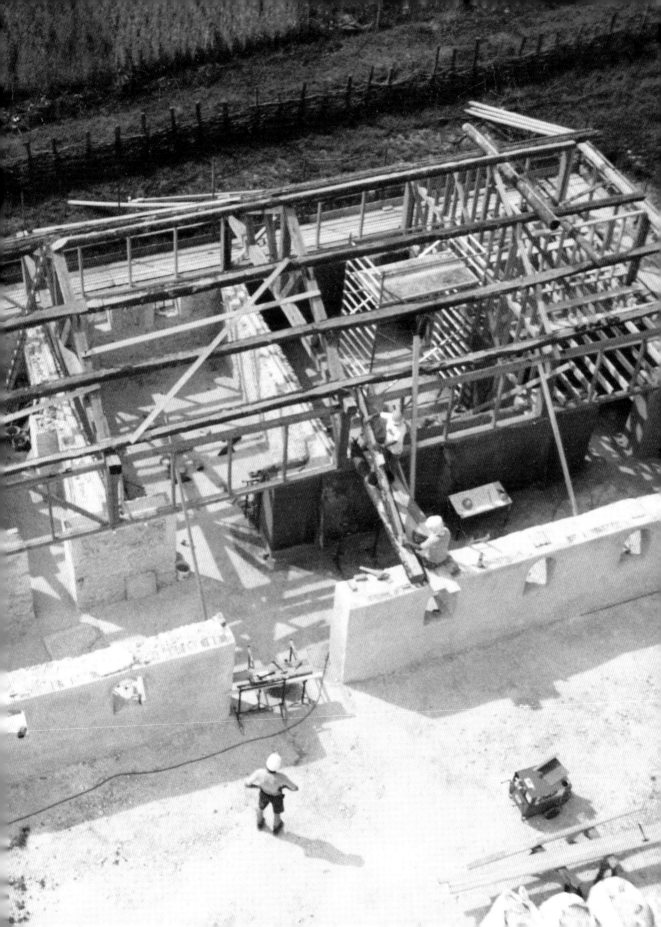

The mosaic discovered at the Sparsholt Roman villa in 1968.

# 7 FLOORED AGAIN

If you ask most people to tell you something about Roman villas, the first thing they will say is that all the floors are bright with mosaics of varying patterns and themes. In fact, this is not the usual case and, leaving aside a couple of exceptions, it is worth noting that most villas have only a very small number of mosaics. The villa at Sparsholt had only two pattern mosaics in the main building and the whole complex produced only another one. This means that we have to consider the other types of flooring which occur in a Roman villa. What we have tried to do with the Butser Roman villa is to show the variety of floor types which were available and might reasonably be found in such a villa. This makes it look a bit like a Roman flooring showroom but we felt that this approach helps both with the experimental and educational aspects of the villa and, in particular, helps us examine the relationship between flooring and the rest of a room and how floors might be experienced. So in the eight rooms of the villa we have six types of flooring. The most obvious type that we have left out is stone paving. We have left this because the area of Hampshire in which our villa is located in is not an area which produces suitable geological deposit of 'flag' or paving stones.

## DOWN TO EARTH

The first type of floor and apparently the simplest is the 'earth' floor. This can take a number of forms. The simplest is what is present when the building has been finished – a sort of 'construction layer' of mud and building debris which can be levelled off. This, as long as it remains dry will provide a reasonable, if dusty floor. It will not wear well especially in areas of more intense use, for example around doorways or working areas. However, it is the sort of level that we will leave in the 'storage' room which forms part of the 'service' suite of rooms.

Then there are a whole set of methods of providing a firmer and better surface which is still 'earth'. We do not know what methods the Romans used. There are no statements about the preparation of

# Mortar and Mosaics . . . by Mel Bliss artist and archaeologist

**AS** an archaeologist, I am no stranger to physical labour, but the Butser villa came with an additional challenge – learning to build a structure which one would usually dig up! I remember the first flint being laid in August 2002, and afterwards, the thrill we got from building two-foot-thick walls of flint and mortar – a process which reminded me of an enormous three dimensional jigsaw puzzle.

I had a rather messy, hands-on technique which became a source of amusement to the team as I encrusted various tools and tea mugs with mortar. But after suffering lime burns on the end of every finger, I evolved my style into a more conventional approach using gloves.

The winter bought many uncertainties about the future of the project, but Steve Terrell and I slogged on, fortified by his winter stews. I devised a monitoring and recording system to ensure completion of the walls by the end of May 2003. Even though a team of five had just ten weeks to erect over half the walls, with the help of my new system, we did it.

Later, I was asked to produce an M. D. F mock-up of a mosaic for the summer dining room. The actual mosaic design found at Sparsholt seemed the obvious model. In choosing a design the Romans must haved considered room function and the personal tastes and spirituality of the home owner not to mention the size of his purse! Each pattern and motif was carefully organized into the desired shape and size. The process made me think about the mosaic 'consultants' that would have worked through these processes (rather like myself with the M. D. F version), designing the patterns well before the painstaking task of cutting and laying of actual tessera which is like a 'painting by numbers' stage requiring more dexterity and patience than artistic ability.

these surfaces in the literature, and the archaeological evidence cannot help because an earth floor with no covering above it will be penetrated by damp, by earthworms and by the roots of trees and vegetation. All these factors will break up and disturb the layers of earth and make it impossible to determine exactly what was going on – literally a case of 'earth to earth'. A number of ways of strengthening earth floors are known because they were in actual use well into the last century and within living memory. Common techniques involve digging over the floor and adding material such as lime, chalk lumps, and cinders including waste material from smithies to it to make it stronger. There is also the famous occasional addition of 'bull's blood' which is said to improve the composition and a protein-based liquid such as milk will help strengthen an earth floor. It is also reported that washing an earthen floor with water and soot will help maintain the durability. The important thing is that the mixture is beaten down hard to produce a smooth surface. The worst thing for the current survival of earthen floors are modern trainers which are designed to grip, they are even worse than spike heels which only penetrate.

Vitruvius mentions a type of floor similar to the ones just described 'as inexpensive and useful'[1] for winter dining rooms. Following Greek fashion you excavate to a depth of two feet, lay a rubble layer, then trampled coals topped by six inches of a mortar mix of gravel, lime and ash. This is then made level and polished with a whetstone so it looks like a black pavement. Vitruvius reports that the great thing about this flooring is that wine that has been spilled or spat out dries quickly and 'those that do the pouring, even if they serve with bare feet, will not catch cold from this type of pavement'.[2] This passage is repeated in Faventius virtually word for word so this type of flooring was still around in AD 300. The suggested usage in a winter dining room shows that this sort of floor could be good enough to be high status, but against this it should be remembered that such a floor could be awful if not maintained. There is a medieval Welsh story called the 'Dream of Rhonabwy' which opens with a group taking shelter in a hall somewhere in Montgomeryshire

> *and when they came inside, they could see a floor full of holes and uneven. Where there was a bump upon it, it was with difficulty a man might stand thereon, so exceeding slippery was the floor with cows' urine and their dung.*[3]

We will not be having animals inside our villa but we need to remember the downside of earthen floors. Lastly we should remember that the surface of the floor could be covered with straw or dried grass in order to protect it. This is a layer which can be swept up and easily laid again.

## MORTAR FLOORS

A type of flooring which is frequently found on Roman sites but tends to be largely ignored in the standard literature is the 'mortar' floor. This consists of a spread of mortar of varying thickness usually applied directly on the earth. This simply hardens up the surface to make it look better and is an approach that can also be used to repair other types of floor when they are damaged or become worn. There is not much that can be said about them but we will be using the technique at the Butser Roman villa in the service/kitchen area.

As we have seen, the earth floor by virtue of its material leaves very little in the way of archaeological traces. The other organic material used for flooring is wood in the form of floorboards. There is now evidence that the Romans did have plank floors laid over joists and

A tessallated floor at Butser Roman villa, October 2003.

nailed down. In the case of timber buildings the joists were attached to the framework of the building. At Dolaucothi, the Roman gold mine in Carmarthenshire, the joists were laid in slots cut into the earth and this is the technique we will be using at Butser. This must lead to rapid rotting of the timber because there is constant contact with the soil but this is something that we will monitor. There is be another problem in that we could be using modern kiln dried timber which will probably not be as long-lasting as Roman timber but we might try examples of both sorts to allow us to compare the results. Of course, although the slots for the joists cut in the ground might show in excavation it is clearly possible that an ordinary earth floor would look much the same archaeologically as an area covered by a plank floor once the planks have decayed.

There is a type of floor whose name occurs frequently in the literature of Roman building techniques called *opus signinum*. As archaeologists now use the term it basically means a mortar mix with added crushed brick or terracotta, including some quite large lumps, but there are some arguments about its exact nature. The name does not help us in deter-mining what the Romans meant: '*opus*' translates as a 'work or construction' and '*signinum*' means after the fashion of Signia, a small town to the south west of Rome. Archaeologists always call it *op. sig.* and there have been many arguments about what this was and its composi-tion. To try to clarify the points at issue let us first begin with Vitruvius.

If we take those explicit references in Vitruvius's *Ten Books on Architecture* to *op. sig.*, the first (Book 2, Chapter 5) 'in describing various building materials' says that because of its fine grain, river sand is useless for *op. sig.* but alright for plasterwork. The fullest reference comes in Book 8, Chapter 6. This section is dealing with water supplies and how to construct waterproof cisterns in which to store water. He says specifically of *op. sig.*

> *First of all, the purest and roughest sand should be readied, and then rubble of silex should be broken up, no heavier than a pound, and mixed as vigorously as possible with lime*

*in a mortar, so that five parts of sand correspond with two
of lime.*[4]

This mixture is then used to construct waterproof cisterns. The word
'*silex*' is a vague term which has no modern equivalent, but the most
recent commentary on Virtuvius suggests that it  probably refers to a
hard limestone. This only goes to emphasise the problems we have in
dealing with technical details from Roman sources. The conclusion is
that by *op. sig.* Vitruvius  meant a waterproof cement not necessarily
for floors and with a specific but unknown ingredient of *silex*.

So what of the *op. sig.* beloved of modern archaeologists? Vitruvius
gives the formula for a form of flooring which contains mortar and
crushed terracotta in Book 7, Chapter 1. Note that the section is in the
context of making floors over an existing wooden decking '*as flawless
as possible*'.

*Then, together with* [two parts of] *fresh rubble, mix a third
part of crushed terracotta, to this mixture lime should be introduced in the mortar in a ratio of two parts to five.*[5]

Vitruvius sees this mixture being laid over an underlayer of fist-sized
rocks to a depth of one foot. Over the mortar and terracotta layer he
recommends a pavement of tesserae or small bricks. He also recommends weatherproofing the mortar against frost by saturating it with
the residue from pressing olive oil. However, nowhere does Vitruvius
explicitly call this mixture '*op. sig.*' and we should note that the propor-
tions of 'fresh rubble' are in square brackets and thus a doubtful part
of the original work.

When we come to Faventius, there are changes. He doesn't talk
about cisterns but transfers the advice to wells. The aggregate should
be the mysterious *silex* or *tufa* and two parts of lime should be mixed
to five of rough sand (as Vitruvius). Faventius then says that practical
experience has found it better to mix one of lime to two of sand. The
cost will be greater but the aggregate will be more firmly bound

together. He then adds that if you want brick-faced concrete you
proceed in exactly the same way. So Faventius does not see the need to
include pounded brick in his *op. sig.* but keeps this for *opus testaceum*
– whatever exactly that is!

So, faced with this confusion, what did we do with *op. sig.* at the
Butser Roman villa? We tried a series of experiments to investigate
the practicality of the mixes and how they are laid. The first
technique, which does not work very well, is to lay the floor 'wet'.
This involves slaking the lime and immediately mixing in the
crushed brick and fragments of brick and tile. This is necessary in
order to have the chemical reaction which binds the brick bits into
the mixture. As has been said, the chemical reaction involves heat
and a physical reaction so while it is possible (with great care) to
mix a small amount and move it in a metal wheelbarrow this would
not work with the wicker baskets that the Romans might have used.
After making a series of test squares the solution arrived at, which
seems to work, is to mix one part lime with three of crushed brick
and tile fragments and a minimal amount of water and then to

pound it into position to consolidate the floor. This mixture will set slowly, making use of the water in the ground, providing a practical downside for this technique as it is estimated that it might take up to one month for the mixture to dry. We have tried a small area and will be doing a larger area but if this approach is correct it will tell us something about the time taken in flooring buildings with *op. sig.*

The *op. sig.* floors should set to a good reddish colour thanks to the crushed brick. Vitruvius and Faventius seem to refer to the 'polishing' of floors presumably with abrasive powders to make them level and a shine can be given to this sort of floor using milk with the whey removed.


## BRICK FLOORS

We now come to the type of floors made of brick in various sizes and other materials with the most elaborate being known as 'mosaics'. Given the extent of Roman tile use in the construction of roofs, *pilae* and wall decoration it is surprising that this material is not used more often in the construction of floors. However, there is a type of paving known as *opus spicatum,* made from small bricks, but less than forty examples are known from Roman Britain. As some of these are from central southern Britain, including Silchester, it was felt appropriate to have an example of this technique in the Butser Roman villa. As with *op. sig.* the *opus* part means 'work', and in this case *spicatum* means 'like an ear of wheat'. This refers to the way the lines of brick are laid in a zigzag pattern. In English we use the fishy analogy of 'herringbone' to describe the pattern. The range of sizes of the bricks used varies greatly with no standardised size but an 'average' size is about fourteen and a half millimetres wide by sixty-three millimetres long and twenty-six millimetres deep. These bricks are laid in lime mortar and the literary sources suggest that when they have been set they might be finished by the application of coats of lime and sand, presumably to protect them. We have tended to assume that the rarity and lack of standardisation of this type of flooring in Britain makes it a bit 'special' and we have used it in the high-status end of the villa as a paving for the ante-room off the corridor. It has also been suggested that *op. spic.* is laid in areas of higher use so the confined space and expected traffic through the ante-room makes it a suitable area for the technique.

## MOSAIC AND TESSALLATED FLOORS

Before looking more closely at tessallated and mosaic pavements it is useful to think briefly about the relative importance that the Romans put on these floors. This can be done by assessing the relative wages paid to the different craftsmen involved. We know these prices for the year AD 301 because by then Emperor Diocletian was trying to stem inflation and produced a price list for goods and also for workers of different types. So, the person who laid the tessallated pavement or simpler mosaic, identified as a *tessellarius,* was rated at fifty denarii per day. The craftsman who did the finer figured mosaics, a *musaearius,* was paid sixty denarii. In relative terms a *tessellarius* was rated to be as skilled as a stonemason, carpenter, blacksmith or baker. The *musaearius* was rated alongside shipwrights. However, those dealing with floors, however elaborate, were more lowly rated and paid than those dealing with wall paintings. An ordinary wall painter was paid seventy denarii but the best painter of figures and scenes, the *pictor imaginarius,* was paid one hundred and fifty denarii or three times the rate of the *tessellarius.*

A fine mosaic at Bignor in West Sussex might give us a clue to the name of a real *musaearius.* There are what appear to be initials reading 'TR' or 'TER' . But they can be expanded in three ways as Terentius, Tertius or Tertullus, so long-lasting fame is somewhat watered down! A recent study has suggested that it is the name of the muse of dancing, TERpsichore or, if a name is split by the design of the mosaic, it could be of one of the classical names of the winds, ausTER. But the fact is that the name sits in its own box not 'in the frame' with the figure, so let us be bold and say that there is one exception to the anonymity of our mosaic craftsmen.

Tessallated pavements are a simpler form of mosaic. They are made out of tesserae (small cubes of brick) set in a matrix of mortar. The

A tessallated floor from
the excavation at
Sparsholt..

tesserae are usually quite large and generally all of one colour with no patterns. I suppose that another way of describing them is mosaics without patterns or pictures. They are laid down as a hard-wearing flexible sort of floor and, because of the time spent in preparing the tesserae and laying the floor, they are an indication of higher but not highest status. In some cases a tessallated pavement is set as the border for the main, finer mosaic. They also occur in corridors and other areas experiencing heavy use.

Let us begin our study of mosaics proper with a definition. According to the *Concise Oxford Dictionary*, mosaics are 'a form or work of art in which pictures or patterns are produced by joining together small pieces of stone, glass etc. of different colours'. In considering the details of mosaics we will look at the materials used and how the mosaicists would have worked.

The tesserae which form the mosaic would mostly have come from local materials. So the colour palette of any mosaic will derive from the locality and each mosaic will have subtle, and not so subtle, differences from other ones independently of all other factors of design and construction. The most common elements forming tesserae are chalk, limestone, brick or terracotta, sandstones and shale. But occasionally, there are materials such as glass, for example in Silchester, Bignor and Clanville in Hampshire, not far from Butser. The villa at Box in Wiltshire had pavements with white limestone, blue-black lias, chocolate-coloured pennant stone, yellow from oolite and red from broken tiles, all coming from within five miles of the villa. The size of the tesserae may also have an influence on the effect of the design or picture. Sizes vary but, for example, from Lufton in Somerset there are two predominant sizes of half and one and a half centimetres square.

One of the mosaics found at Sparsholt nicely illustrates the local sourcing of materials. This is the one in the central reception/summer dining room. The colours used are red, grey, white and yellow with varying shades. What is unusual is that the colour yellow is limited in its use only to the central flower. Where you might have expected yellow in the guilloche (a form of interwoven linear decoration), the border and the secondary motifs, a pale grey has been substituted. This is presumably because of the difficulty of obtaining yellow stone locally.

The time spent in laying mosaics was significant as was the amount of material needed. The modern reproduction of the Great Pavement at

Detail from the edge of
the mosaic at Sparsholt.

Making tesserae
Roman-style by
breaking up large
cubes of terracotta
with a hammer and a
sharp metal edge.

Woodchester took place at the rate of two square feet a day using a third-inch square tesserae. A more recent reconstruction of part of a mosaic at Basildon Berkshire for the Channel 4's *Time Team* was also interesting. A wooden tray of 1.2 metres square was made together with a mortar bed. This followed Vitruvius with one part of lime mortar with three parts crushed brick and some sand. Blue-grey lias was used for the outline, hard chalk for the infilling (while softer than limestone, chalk is a better white), tiles for red and a brownish-yellowish ironstone for the fourth colour. The whole of one day and part of another was spent producing the tesserae, even with the help of electric saws, but this size panel required approximately 12,500 cubes. While the team laying the mosaic were relatively inexperienced, and the time taken to lay this area was about fourteen hours and the conclusion was that a three-metre square panel could be easily laid in a week. However, it was also concluded that as much, if not more time would be spent in making the tesserae. It is suggested that tesserae-making might have been a winter activity of the mosaic craftsmen so as to have a supply in hand. Mosaics were clearly valued, there was even one in London which was protected in situ while the building it was in was demolished around it and rebuilt. The basic conclusion is that these are expensive items and, in modern terms, we should be thinking in terms of five to six figure sums depending upon the elaboration and size.

How to start the laying of a mosaic? For the best results rubble should be laid down and consolidated. It should then be covered by a layer of *op. sig.*, This could be an existing floor which has been laid perhaps with the long-term plan that it would form the basis for a mosaic at some time. If it is an old floor then a new mortar mix will have to be laid to take the tesserae. However, there are examples where

Tesserae are glued onto a sheet upon which the pattern is marked out.

Christine Shaw making
the mosaic for the
hypocaust room,
September 2003.

the *op. sig.* mortar has been laid straight on the earth without any
further preparation. There is evidence that the basic pattern of the
mosaic is then either scored in the mortar or the guidelines are painted
or lined in. Work on the mosaic probably starts from the centre of the
room progressing out to the border. The main motifs are laid first,
followed by the background tesserae and guilloche later.

There are several methods of setting tesserae into the bed of mortar.
The direct method is the most probable one for many sites and
elements. This involves the tesserae being set directly into the mortar
without any preparation beforehand – a sort of freehand approach.
This clearly leads to mistakes, for example, in the guilloche. In laying

out the guilloche it is suggested that the 'eye' is placed first and then the rest laid around. If the 'eye' is wrongly located adjustments have to be made further around the pattern to make it fit.

The next method is the indirect method. The great advantage of this is that it can be prefabricated off-site, either a short distance or further away. In the indirect method the tesserae are laid down in a supportive material such as sand. On the constructed pattern strong pieces of material are then glued onto the surface. The sort of glue used would be an animal glue made from boiling bones. This holds the pattern in place and the sheet could be rolled up and then laid down in the place reserved for it, presumably in a mortar bed. Once this has set, the glue can be dissolved with hot water, the sheet lifted off and the mosaic cleaned up. Mistakes can happen with this technique if measurements are not correct. A well-known example is from Verulamium where a prefabricated lion attacking a stag was not centred properly so, although the stag's horns are complete, the lion has had the end of his tail cut off by the needs of a regular border. It is quite clear that the mosaicists did not always get it right. What is interesting is that the patrons or owners of the villas seem to have either accepted the mistakes or not 'seen' them.

There is further evidence for some use of the indirect method for laying mosaics from the mosaics at Hinton St Mary (Dorset) and Rudston (Yorkshire). In the former there were dark streaks in the mortar bed indicating prefabrication and in the latter the types of mortar varied from the motifs to the borders.

A variant of the direct method is the 'reverse' method. In this the tesserae are glued face down onto a cloth, which could have the desired picture or pattern drawn onto it. The same procedure would be followed as for the indirect method but when the mosaic panel was in position it would be 'back to front' from the way it had been constructed. It has been suggested that this technique is responsible for 'wrong' or mirror images in mosaics. For example, a figure which usually carries something on its right shoulder can be shown carrying it on its left. But the debate about which of the various methods of laying mosaics were

Detail of the mosaic a Sparsholt showing the *guilloche* edging pattern and the symbol of a *cantharus* drinking vessell. The black and white scale shows the size in centimetres.

used in Roman Britain is ongoing and it now seems that it is probable that the indirect reverse method was not used. It is probable that the majority of mosaics in Roman Britain were laid on site.

The next question to consider is the designs in the mosaics. There are similarities in design, motifs and themes between some mosaics. It has been suggested that in some cases these are close enough to form 'schools' or workshops of mosaic designers and workers who operated in geographically restricted areas. These areas often seem to hinge upon the presence of a significant Roman administrative/political centre with the clients or patrons of the mosaic schools being the elite based on such centres. For example, in

A simple spiral pattern
from the tessallated
floor of the Sparsholt
villa corridor.

southern England 'schools' have been postulated based in Cirencester (Corinium – a provincial capital), and the Roman towns at Dorchester, Dorset, Ilchester, Silchester, and (near to our site) Winchester. It also seems that some motifs or 'themes' occurring on mosaics might tie in with long standing cultural (even tribal) divisions existing in Roman Britain. However, if it is accepted that some form of 'pattern books' existed, which seems to be the case, this would allow for the transmission of ideas and the Roman 'gentry' visiting each other's villas would derive inspiration in 'following' – or kicking against – the Jones's or their Roman equivalent's taste in mosaics. Rather than an ordered semi-centralised mosaic craft industry it could be that, depending on who and what money was available, it was a bit of a 'mix and match' with mosaic designers, a few master-craftsmen and more jobbing semi-skilled workmen all involved in the process at different levels. If you can only afford the cheaper mosaic workers then their advice, as well as quality of execution, would be different from that of a top-rate master mosaicist. The final say was probably with the person who commissioned the mosaic, which need not necessarily have been the owner, or members of their family, of course, but some sort of 'taste guru' such as valued slave or freedman.

Portrait of Christ from the Hinton St Mary mosaic in the British Museum.

Where mosaics have clear themes in their decoration there has been much debate about the level of meaning that might be found in them. At one level there are 'simple' themes such as the presence of a *cantharus* or drinking vessel. This might indicate that the room it was in was perhaps a dining room. Bathhouses often have themes to do with water such as fish. But there are then the wider use of mythological subjects – the representations of the Roman gods and goddesses and events from Virgil's *Aeneid*. The *Aeneid* was the touchstone of the civilised Rome and provided the 'foundation myth' for the Roman world. On the one hand, the parade of Roman deities and mythology might simply indicate the wish of the villa owner to demonstrate how well educated he was, as well as giving a suitable subject for discussion with his peer group. On the other hand, it has been argued that these themes might be related to late Roman mystery religions and that some villas were not only homes and public reception places but could also be a centre for groups of like-minded people joining in pagan and – as we shall come to – Christian worship; ceremonies would place not in some separate temple but in the villa itself in a room which had been decorated with this function in mind. By worship we must remember that this could involve not just some ritual recognition of a particular god but also a more social side with associated feasting and drinking. With this in mind it is worth noting that Bacchus, the god of wine and the lord of salvation, plays a significant role in various Romano-British mosaics.

A few mosaics feature elements of Christian iconography. The Hinton St Mary (Dorset) mosaic in the British Museum shows a male head in the central roundel with a symbol known as a 'chi-rho' (standing for the first two letters of Christ in Greek) behind the head. This head is generally accepted to be that of Christ and the chi-rho occurs on a very few other sites. What is perhaps more difficult to accept and understand is the idea that mosaic pictures of pagan classical themes can also be regarded as having a Christian meaning. For example, at Frampton (Dorset) a chi-rho is set centrally in front of an apse. The mosaics which decorate the rooms on the approach to the apse feature Bacchus, hunting scenes (which can be viewed as the quest for the truth as well as a popular sport), Bellerophon seated on Pegasus killing the Chimera (which can be seen as the victory of good over evil) and so on. It is probable that the form of Christianity that was being practised in parts of late Roman Britain was syncretic, that is, it was combining beliefs from several religions. This is just a small taster of the debate surrounding the interpretation of mosaics which is large and ongoing. It is fair to say that there are some eminent people studying mosaics who feel that the search for meaning is too extreme and not very profitable.

The final thing to discuss about mosaics is their positioning in a room. For example, it has been suggested that a broad band of plain tessalated pavement at the back of a room might be where the couches for dining were placed. The mosaic in the same room would then be expected to be aligned in that direction so the diners reclining on the couches might have the benefit of the best view. There are other cases where unexplained areas of tessallated pavement within an elaborate scheme challenge us to think about why they occur. Could it be where large items of furniture were placed or other static items such as statues? We can never be sure, but this question does add to the challenge of trying to sort out how Roman rooms worked.

At the Butser Roman villa we are making the first mosaic for the 'winter dining room'. The theme in the middle panel will be an ear of corn to reflect the corn growing basis of the presumed wealth of the owners and also the agricultural interests of Butser Ancient Farm. The surrounding motifs and borders are all taken from local Hampshire mosaics. We prefabricated large areas of the central panel and laid the coarser borders in situ. The colour range has been chosen to reflect the limited use of yellow on the Sparsholt mosaic. Red comes from tile, black from tile fired without oxygen, white and grey from local stones . In the room 'library' next to the winter dining room, we have laid a simple tessallated pavement with plain red cubes. In the reception/summer dining room we have 'made' mosaics (in the plural) out of painted board so that we can change some of the themes in the mosaic to show how they might be 'read' – for example a chi-rho may be incorporated to show that the owner has perhaps become a Christian.

The completed mosaic in Butser, October 2003.

The completed paintings and M. D. F. mosaic in the summer dining room of Butser Roman villa, October 2003.

# POOR
# TASTE IN
# PAINTINGS

P ainters, as we have seen when we looked at mosaics, held the highest status among those craftsmen associated with buildings. But it is a bit artificial to divide paintings from mosaics: they would both have been viewed as part of the overall decorative plan. When thinking about paintings, as with mosaics, we need to consider what colours were available, the techniques used and schemes of decoration including the themes involved. We will also be looking at how the exterior might have been decorated and as we will see, modern tastes might find it a touch 'in your face'.

This is what Faventius has to say about painting:

> for any walls that are diligently finished are unaffected by old age, and never lose the beauty of their colour when cleaned. For when walls that are still damp are adorned with paintings, they will dry out and the colour that is rooted in the fabric cannot be washed away[1]

and:

> winter dining rooms are not suitable for decoration with large pictures, for they are quickly dulled by the smoky light from candles or lamps, which have to be numerous in winter. So, too, their vaults have flat surfaces, so that one can wipe the smoke off them and restore them to their brightness.[2]

And beyond written details of the pigments used, that is almost the sum total of the written record on wall paintings. So before we look at what Faventius's 'large pictures' might have consisted of let us look at the techniques involved.

## GETTING PLASTERED

The surface of the wall must be prepared prior to painting. We looked at the early stages of plastering in the chapter on walls but if the wall is to be painted then preparation can be more complex and the number of coats of plaster that need to be built up before painting starts can vary. Vitruvius, writing from a perfectionist metropolitan point of view, argues for seven coats of plaster with an initial rough coat to help later coats adhere, then three coats incorporating sand followed by three upper coats incorporating marble dust. In the allied context of plastering ceilings he allows that marble dust can be alternated with a product called *creta* which is generally accepted to be

Plastering the ante-room ceiling, September 2003.

chalk, so that's good news for Butser where marble is in short supply and chalk plentiful. Vitruvius also recognises that he is probably asking for the impossible with seven coats of plaster except in the very best circles, but warns that problems may arise if only two coats are used – one with sand and one with the powdered marble or chalk. At Pompeii three coats seems to be the norm, using two with sand and one with marble dust. A study of Roman wall-painting in Britain indicates that usually only two coats of plaster were used. Generally these consisted of a first coat of three to five centimetres thick and a finishing coat 0.75 cm to 1.3 cm thick. At Butser we will be experimenting with a variety of layers and trying some areas with marble dust and some with chalk powder.

We will also be dealing with redecoration, so it is worth noting at this stage that previously painted plaster can be keyed by pecking the existing surface with something like a small pickaxe. This will mean that the next coat of plaster will engage with the old surface.

## THE ROMAN PALETTE

When it comes to the nature of the paints or pigments used, we have some archaeological help from Britain. This is useful because we do not want to rely too much on evidence from Pompeii and literary sources. Containers with pigments in them have been found which *seem* to show a full range of colours, but scientific analysis has given us a palette of colours that we *definitely* know were being used in Britain:

White    calcium carbonate, probably chiefly from chalk.
Black    carbon from soot or charcoal.
Blue     blue frit or Egyptian blue, a coarse grained glassy pigment containing copper calcium silicate.
Yellow   hydrated ferric oxide known as yellow ochre.
Green    'green earth' which occurs naturally, obtained from Cornwall in medieval times.
Red      most commonly anhydrous ferric oxide found as haematite or red ochre. A site in York has produced evidence of cinnabar or vermilion which is expensive and rare.

Other colours can be produced by mixing these pigments – green and yellow produce brown, red and blue produce purple and so on. Remember that these pigments had to be prepared by hand – ground to a powder in a pestle and mortar – there wouldn't be any suppliers of paint in tubes for many hundreds of years.

## BRUSHING-UP

How about the actual painting? The basic method that seems to have been used is called 'fresco'. The pigments are applied while the plaster is still damp and are firmed up and consolidated by a chemical reaction as water mixed with the pigment and the plaster evaporates bringing lime to the surface. This forms a layer of lime-water over the whole area which dries into a smooth transparent layer. It appears in some cases that the painter actually presses the painted area with some sort of flat board to bring extra fluid to the surface, if you have ever tried plastering you will recognise this phenomenon. The end result is a sort of 'wipe-downable' wall covering – not quite wallpaper but going in that direction. So, fresco is more than just painting on a surface it is also about making the surface tough and cleanable. Wet fresco is known as *fresco buon*.

When we study Roman fresco wall paintings closely we can see in some cases that the plaster was wet when the pigment was applied. We know this because you can not only see the brush strokes in the paint but also see that the bristles caused marks in the plaster. There are other cases where imperfections in the plaster are caused by the painters themselves touching it while they were working.

If the painting and plaster was dry or if, for example, you wanted to repair an area which might have cracked or been damaged by rough contact then you had two choices. You could stick to fresco but in this case dry fresco or *fresco secco* where the pigments are mixed into their own lime-water to fix them on the wall.

The other way is to use some sort of medium which would stick or glue the pigments to the surface. This is known as 'tempera'. The word tempera is not very helpful as it comes from the Latin 'to mix or regulate' and could apply to any mixture of pigment and medium. The medium to be mixed with the pigment needs to be one that will effectively stick the pigment to the surface. There seem to be a number of possible candidates for the 'sticky medium' in Roman times. One of the most commonly used mediums is egg. Its use in the Roman period is mentioned by Pliny and also shown in analysis of some of the portrait masks found on Roman mummies in Egypt. Eggs consist of two parts – the yolk which is an emulsion of fatty material suspended in protein in water and the white which is only protein in water with no fat. A paint containing both yolk and white will include a high proportion of protein and will dry to a more brittle finish than if only the yolk is used since the higher proportion of fat plasticises the paint. This sort of paint dries first by the evaporation of the water and then by the setting of the egg protein. The evaporation of the water considerably reduces the volume of the paint and this means that it cannot

Madeleine Allison painting frescos in the summer dining room, September 2003.

be applied thickly or else it may crack and flake. So the technique is to paint with repeated thin applications. This form of fresco is more fragile than the 'wet plaster' approach.

Other mediums are also possible. Analysis of some wall paintings shows that beeswax might have been used and evidence from Pliny suggests that animal glue is another alternative. It is even possible to use stale beer but no archaeological evidence of this has been found and while it is hoped to carry out experiments using all these media the prospect of beer being allowed to go stale on the Butser site is a possible problem!

However, the remark by Faventius, which repeats Vitruvius, that wet plaster fresco lasts better because the 'colour . . . cannot be washed way,'[3] suggests that there were Roman wall paintings where the colour could be washed away so the techniques of 'tempera' or dry fresco techniques must have been practised but their relative fragility means that they will not have survived very well in the archaeological record.

When painting in fresco the general rule seems to be to start from the top and work down. Roman schemes of decoration are often in horizontal layers which tends to assist this but vertical joins in paintings are also found. There is evidence for guidelines and preliminary sketches outlined on the existing plaster layer either in red ochre, by scoring into the plaster with a pointed instrument or by twanging a taut chalked line onto the plaster to give longer straight lines.

In wet fresco, once the surface had been prepared the plasterer would be rapidly followed by the artist or artists. In fine work there would have been a distinction between the figure or scene painter and the background or ornament painter. In less demanding work there still may have been more than one artist. But given that once the plaster layer has dried it needs to be prepared again, the technique does call for speed and concentration – as well as good teamwork between the plasterer and painters.

Painters need brushes and while we have no archaeological evidence of any complete brushes we know from the marks in the

Fresco from the
Verulamium Museum
in St Albans.

wet plaster that brushes were definitely used. The bone handles of some brushes have turned up on some sites, and from Roman graves in France and Germany we have artists' sets of equipment which were buried with them. Pliny tells us that pigs bristle was used for plasterers' brushes so these, presumably plus finer hairs, could also have been used by Roman painters. Paint containers seem to have been at hand, often using old part-broken pots especially the bases. There is also evidence for the use of larger flatter pieces of broken pottery as palettes along with oyster shells.

## OLD MASTERS

There is evidence for the insertion of prepared panels of paintings into decorative schemes. This is for two reasons. The first is probably the

137

prefabrication of panels off-site comparable to similar practices with-mosaics. The second is the preservation for re-use of elements of earlier wall paintings – a bit like having 'old masters' hanging on your walls – which shows the value placed on paintings as works of art even if they were not quite as portable as free-hanging paintings. Evidence for these practices is found in the survival of wooden frames around certain elements in the walls – in one case, at Herculaneum, the

## A Divine Comedy ... by Madeleine Allison artist

**THE** virgin walls of a unique design from antiquity, set in the beautiful downlands of Hampshire – an artist in Paradise! But every brushstroke to be quickly sealed into the walls by a fine layer of crystelline calcium carbonate – every blemish immortalised – an artist in Purgatory? This became more and more apparent to me as the nature of the *buon fresco* process was revealed. Those ancient alchemists of colour have persistantly refused to give up the secrets of their stunning skills to the modern archeologist and practitioner.

There are acres of paper devoted to the content of Roman wall paintings, but only a few pages on how their spells may have been cast. The occult nature of these processes, therefore, was a gifted challenge for the kind of experimental archaeology that has been the emblem of research at Butser Ancient Farm.

The freshness and power of true fresco, with its raw earth pigments, ground sometimes from semi-precious stones, has enchanted artists throughout the ages. I travelled to Courbieres to study fresco with Ian Harper, a master of the art. As I stood in front of his wall, under the noonday sun in his courtyard, he announced that the figure in the summer dining room of the villa, originally intended to be Pandora was now Ceres, Roman goddess of the corn and good harvests. But Pandora was not to be usurped lightly from her subterranean seat of power. Over those few days we were delivered of a mighty storm; scorpions arrived in the kitchen sink; fires swept down from the hills; blood flowed over the floor from a cut in my foot and bats arrived nightly to swoop around our beds. But Ceres conquered sweetly in the end, and I brought home honey, *millefleurs*, *fleurs des forets*, and *fleurs des montaignes* for friends who had been unwell, and also the confidence I was looking for to start on those beautiful walls.

Knowing how significant the images could be, I chose them carefully. Most of them speak for themselves, the rest are portraits dedicated to the many hearts and hands that went into the fabric of this incredible building. I could go on painting here for years ...

charred remains of a frame were found, otherwise it is the voids that survive. Further evidence comes from the representation in paint of wood frames; from literature where Pliny says that panels were cut out of the walls of the temple of Ceres in Rome to be reset when restoration was completed and in some cases the cutting out in antiquity of emblems from walls. The sites of Pompeii and Herculaneum are helpful in providing evidence for all this as they were overwhelmed by

Roman-style portrait of the late Peter Reynolds, founder of Butser Ancient Farm, from the hypocaust room.

A section of the wall painting from the North Street villa in Lecestershire.

disasters when work was still in progress. In Herculaneum seven panels cut out of a wall painting were found stacked and ready for re-use.

### DECORATIVE SCHEMES

The construction of wall paintings poses many challenges, a British example of these comes from the Norfolk Street villa in Leicestershire. The date of the wall paintings was probably in the late third century. Archaeologists discovered the remains of plaster from a partition wall which had collapsed into a cellar. The wall had been made of unbaked clay bricks bonded together with wet clay (as discussed in the chapter on walls). Two stages of decoration were represented on the walls and the earlier plaster was made ready for the later stage by pecking with a small axe or other tool. While one scheme was quite simple there was also a rather more elaborate scheme. The main zone of was composed of alternate large panels of red and green separated by illusionistic columns, entwined with vine scrolls and Corinthian style capitals. This lay below an imitation classical frieze with a floral frieze above it. Below the main zone was a pale yellow band and then a series of smaller panels, alternatively long and short, painted in imitation marbling above a splashed pink baseboard. From the top corner of the red panels hung green garlands painted as small green blotches close together. Within one of the main panels was a small 'picture' panel of a possible landscape, set within a wide yellow frame. This looks like one of the wooden 'framed' pictures described above. The quality of the plaster seemed to vary from place to place, for example, the pink baseboard has a coarser texture. The fact that the plaster was applied in different stages leading to visible join lines was also noted. The evidence was for two

Detail from the summer dining room mural, September 2003.

clear stages. The plaster for the red panels, columns and the frieze was painted first with the basic colour and perhaps all of the decorative details. The second stage was the green panel and the lower part of the wall. The probable length of the wall was 7.2 metres, so would take a while to paint, but we cannot be sure whether the two stages represent different days' work – making two days in all. There is also conflicting evidence for the technique employed. The work in sections suggests true wet fresco but the flaking off of the paint in some areas shows that proper bonds were not achieved.

## CHANGING ROOMS

We have already considered the high status that painters enjoyed and to this was added the edict of the emperor Valentinian in AD 374 which gave teachers of painting exemptions from taxes, rent free public accommodation and the right to live in whichever town they liked – all very valuable concessions. But who chose the designs and made the choice of what was put on the walls? We have seen that paintings can be graded in complexity, that there is a wide variety of compositional approaches and elements all tied in with the speed of work required by fresco which leads to spontaneity. As Professor Roger Ling author of several works on Roman painting and mosaics says:

> all these elements . . . were determined by social conditions. And the most important conclusion of all is that wall-painting was socially necessary. Any householder with aspirations to a degree of respectability felt obliged to commission murals in at least the most important rooms in his house.[4]

So choice would vary according to what the owner wanted to express and the advice (perhaps based on pattern books) and skills that the painter could bring to the task. And, while the patron had the ultimate choice, decisions on the details of the work would have been a complicated one.

What would our hypothetical 'owner' commission for the Butser Roman villa? Rather like the floors we have gone for a variety of treat-

Detail from the hunting mural in the corridor.

ments and techniques which we can monitor over the next few years to see how they survive and what happens to them. The reception/summer dining room has the most elaborate paintings done mostly in wet fresco. The main figure at the back is of Ceres representing the corn harvest which made the presumed owner wealthy. There is also illusionistic architectural and garden decoration or *trompe l'oeil*.

In other rooms we have portraits in 'wooden' frames and simpler blocks of colour. As you enter the ante-room to the private block you will see a picture of Bacchus, and the corridor will be full of movement

Detail from the figure of Ceres representing the corn harvest in the summer dining room.

with a hunting scene. Many of the human faces will be modelled on people who have worked on the villa.

In the kitchen/service room to the right of the fireplace is a niche for the household shrine. Such shrines are usually associated with hearths and cooking areas. The niche will contain a cast bronze statuette of the 'genius' – a concept which is a mixture of the head of the household and the Emperor. A genius will also be painted at the back of the niche. Later on either side and below will be the 'lares et penates', those who look after the household. These consist traditionally of two figures,

144

one on either side and a serpent underneath. We are following examples from Pompeii.

## PAINTING THE OUTSIDE

We have already discussed why the outside of the Butser Roman villa took its final form. Essentially it came about through following the Luxembourg models and the need to follow modern planning guidance. However the Luxembourg models are not in colour, or if they were painted this has gone, but we need to consider the colours

The household shrine complete with 'genius' in the kitchen.

and any painted schemes which might have decorated the outside of the sort of villa that we are building. As archaeologists, we tend to think very much in monochrome, but this would probably not have been the case with Roman buildings.

We start with two basic colours – the grey of the slates on the main roof, and the white plaster and limewash of the walls. Before looking at other areas to be coloured and the sorts of colours are there any other architectural features that should be added?

For a start we really should have columns flanking the main

entrance to emphasise and reinforce the 'classical' statement made by the pediment of the porch roof. A pediment of this sort, common in classical form of temples, implies the use of columns. Columns would have been very familiar to the villa owners and would have been a common sight in the local town especially around the forum or main administrative complex. Small columns are also used on buildings either along porticoes or verandas and as decoration such as flanking the windows in the Meonstoke façade. So the villa will eventually have columns – what type, we will think about shortly. On the front of the villa there is then very little more that we can add but we should remember that if the villa owner had been really rich, and the stone was available, he would no doubt have built in ashlar or coursed stone blocks. This would have included the

Painted front of the villa with fake stone blocks painted on. The Romans often faked architectural features in paint to give the impression of a high-status building.

windows so they would ideally have been surrounded by nicely cut stones with a key stone at the top and perhaps some decoration such as rosettes.

Archaeology offers some clues which suggest that Roman villa buildings might have been brightly coloured. There are, in Britain, surviving indications of red-painted exterior walls and, at the temple at Lydney in Gloustershire, the plaster had been painted light green with black speckling in a crude attempt to imitate marble. More frequently the colour scheme seems to have involved a strip of colour at the bottom of the wall with white above. Roofs could be decorated with more than the basic 'natural' colours described above for our villa. At the villa at Piddington (Northamptonshire), the tiles were laid with blue imbrices laid over cream tegulae. The colour effects

were achieved by varying the type of firing in the kilns. Also at Piddington the portico had red columns with white details to indicate the bases and capitals (tops) and a subsidiary corridor pierced by windows had its exterior face painted with vertical stripes about one metre wide in sequence – plum-red, white, khaki, white and pale green.

So how do we treat the front of the Butser Roman villa? To the Roman owner it would be a strong statement of his position and it should be possible to 'read' it as such in the landscape. If we use paint we can vary the approaches to the colour schemes. So, eventually, the doorway will have a column on either side but they will be painted onto the whitewashed walls in red. At a later date we might go for real columns but perhaps made out of mudbrick which can be carved to the round and then plastered. Alternatively we might use wood, also painted. Under usual circumstances neither material would leave archaeological traces so columns could easily disappear from the archaeological record. The flat front of the pediment is also picked out and emphasised. The 'order' used for the columns will be the 'Tuscan' one with a flat capital and base. Other orders, which are more elaborate, could be considered, especially the Corinthian one with its top modelled on the flower of the acanthus, but the Tuscan feels right to start with. Then, for the rest of the wall, we could go for some of the more elaborate schemes but to start with we are following the idea of making the villa look as if it has been made out of cut stone blocks. So the plaster will be whitewashed and 'pretend' blocks of stone picked out in red paint. The windows and the corners will be done first then the main body of the wall. On the sides and back we are painting the main walls in whitewash and picking out the beams and woodwork in red. So although the walls are made out of rough flints they have been made to look like something grander – a conceit that is very human and not just confined to the Roman elite.

So, now we have painted our villa inside and out it is time to add a few finishing touches . . .

Detail from the pastoral mural in the summer dining room.

The Roman villa and Iron Age roundhouse at Butser Ancient Farm, October 2003.

# FINISHING TOUCHES

This final chapter considers the control of the openings into and within the villa. It starts with windows, moves to doors and then, because of the question of curtains, moves logically on to a Roman view of feasting. If the logic escapes you at the moment don't worry, it will become clear, and anyway logic is really a Greek rather than a Roman concept.

## A WINDOW ON THE (ROMAN) WORLD

We have already looked at the question of window shapes in the section on walls. Two sorts were decided on, round-headed openings on the front of the villa and square windows on the back and one side. We have no surviving evidence of actual window frames or shutters from Roman Britain. We have some glass which we are pretty certain came from windows and we have some iron window grilles and associated bits of metalwork. There are also some hinges which could have been small enough to be associated with windows rather than doors – or they could be for cupboards so we have tried to take the limited evidence available, use guidance from elsewhere in the Roman world and use some hunches based on medieval practices. So as you can see, we are skating on even thinner ice than usual. We are also guessing at the reaction of the Roman occupants to cold and draughts, not to mention their expectations of what light was needed to live by.

We have given timber frames to the round-headed windows on to the corridor. We have used known Roman joints and the frames will take wooden round-headed shutters. As I have said there is no firm evidence for these but it seems a reasonable way to fill the shape and to provide a method of keeping out the cold and reducing heat loss. Because of the depth of the walls we are having them open to the front. Again, there is no evidence, but it seems logical. These shutters will be painted to form part of the exterior colour scheme.

We decided to treat the square windows in different ways to experiment with a number of possiblities. In the hypocaust room there are smaller windows to the rear of the villa and built into the lower wall.

These are timber framed but have panes of glass mortared into them. This heated room would have been really rather dark and the lack of openings to the outside would have made it fairly airless but this would be the price to be paid for being warm. The 'library', has two grounfloor openings which illustrate examples of the sort of metal window grilles that have been found on archaeological sites. There is an wrought iron grill that has a square framework with iron 'stars' partly filling in the gaps. This copies several examples including the one found at the Hinton St Mary villa in Dorset. There is also an alternative form to fit those cases where the iron stars alone have been

Iron window grille ready for the lower rear windows of the villa.

found. In this type the square frame is made of wood with the stars added to the bars. When painted, the two types would not have appeared too different. This type of design, set firmly into the wall, would have kept out human and also larger mammals and birds. Smaller mammals and birds would have been able to get in so security is presumably the main consideration – with a decorative edge. These windows have been given square shutters, set inside the grilles and opening inwards to cut out the weather and reduce draughts.

The reception/summer dining room originally had three ground floor windows. But once we had experienced the half-built room it was decided to block these up to make a blank wall with all the emphasis on the wide doorway – at the back there are two higher level smaller windows.

The kitchen/service room has three windows. Two of these have simple metal grilles, copying examples from Verulamium. The third window has a grill made out of fired clay with holes in it. Grilles could also have been made out of wood. Their main purpose is to cut down human and animal intruders. We have broad examples of such forms

Clay window grille in from one of the kitchen windows.

from elsewhere in the Roman world. These windows also have internal wooden shutters.

With the upper windows we have gone for simple shutters which can be closed from ground level but this is based on absolutely no evidence whatsoever. There may be the need to add wooden grilles to control birds – but would the Romans have worried?

So, with window fittings we can control the access of various mammals and birds, we can allow light and air in and we can, with

Making glass windows
for the hypocaust room,
September 2003.

shutters, keep it out – to a limited extent. But shutters are either open or closed and there are other things which could have happened without leaving archaeological traces. The first is that draughts could have been limited and a level of light allowed in by means of some sort of membrane set in a frame in the opening. Not glass, but maybe an animal membrane stretched tight or perhaps oiled linen. The other approach is that, for the winter, the openings could have been sealed up entirely – as happened, and still happens in some areas, as a defence against the Russian winter. We can be aware of these ideas, even experiment with them and look again at the archaeological evidence to see if something new might turn up.

We do have a better idea of how window glass was made. Glassmaking is a skilled process which needs craftsmen. Glass is a mixture

# Daub and Doors . . .  by **David Freeman** archaeological interpreter

**I WAS** asked by Christine Shaw to lead a team to daub the wattle panels of the villa because I had been renovating Butser's Iron Age roundhouses and knew the local materials. Christine asked me, even before the first shovel full, how long it would take, and, when pushed for a time, I told her two and a half to three weeks.

I adopted the cement mixer as a daub slave, and named it 'Servius Rotatum', which translates as 'to entwine and rotate'. I also checked for an appropriate deity, and discovered Mepheris, goddess of foul smells and swamps, so that was settled.

Servius Rotatum worked overtime, with no tea breaks for many days. A full load took half an hour to assemble, mix and barrow away (filling two to three barrows a go). In two and a half weeks, we made and plastered twenty tons of daub which was duly thrown, slapped and shovelled onto the walls. The smile on Christine's face was worth it!

The task of designing and constructing the doors was a different challenge. There were four internal doors, one external pair and eight pairs of shutters to work through. The shutters took thirty-two metres of wood, and were painted inside and out in a lime based paint, while the internal doors were of different designs to cover alternative Roman techniques. The front doors were the biggest challenge and I had many nights of disturbed sleep while designing them. A pair of high-status, panelled English oak doors, in an oak frame and decorated with brass studs now adorn the front of the building.

of silica, soda and lime. 'Silica' – in simple terms: sand – forms about sevnty-five per cent of the total mix, fifteen per cent soda is aded as a flux to speed the fusing of the mixture and the final ten per cent is lime (once again) to act as stabiliser. Impurities in the mixture affect the colour of the glass. For example, iron in the sand makes the glass a bluish green. Old broken glass called 'cullet' added in a proportion of fifteen to thirty per cent of the mixture will lower the temperature at which fusion happens and this technique would have been available to Roman glass-makers. It has been said that Roman window glass was first made by casting the molten glass into rectangular wooden moulds. This sort of glass is glossy or 'fire-polished' on one side and pitted with a matt finish on the other and thickness varies within the same piece of glass. But there are several hints within the glass that casting was not the actual technique used. Besides the varying depth there are sometimes tool marks present on the glass and casting does not seem to be the answer for the forms of the edges and corners. Experiments have taken place which replicate the marks found in Roman window glass. The technique takes molten glass, pours it onto a damp wooden surface and flattens it with a block of damp wood.

This produces a disk of glass. This disk is then reheated and pulled into a rectangular shape, using pincers and iron rods to hold the glass in position. The straightness of the sides can be adjusted with heating and pulling with hooks. This technique is straightforward and can be repeated. Later in the Roman period window glass was made more simply and with less need for manipulation by blowing a cylinder of molten glass then gathering the glass and swinging it from a blowing iron, just like making glass vessels. The ends are then opened, and it is cut, reheated and opened out flat. This gives window glass which is glossy on both sides.

## BEHIND CLOSED DOORS

The other openings which control access are, of course, the doorways. Leaving the main doorway for the moment, there are seven others in the interior with differing characteristics. After looking at the archaeological evidence for doors we will see how they might 'fit' and then decide what else might be considered. We do have some doors surviving from Roman Britain. Most show the crudity of Roman timber construction and consist of vertical planks with two sets of horizontal 'ties', called 'ledges', nailed to hold the construction together. They are very much like a modern shed door although even those have diagonal pieces of wood across the ledges to 'brace' the door. One Roman military example has this

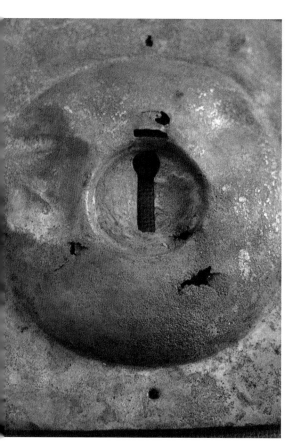

Roman door lock found at Brading villa on the Isle of Wight.

cross-bracing but on the archaeological evidence available in southern England, the 'simple' sort of door will be one of the types used at Butser. The other sort of interior door we will use is a sort of folding door found in the Dewlish villa made from three oak boards with horizontal ledges and hooked iron hinges. These two types will fit four of the doorways, but there is evidence that the Romans also used curtains in doorways so we will use those for the other three and you can read more about Roman curtains later on.

What do we do with the front door? In Butser we are following the archaeology of examples from Pompeii. The front doors are to be double leaved (stable doors) which open outwards. They are panelled with bracing but the carpentry is still fairly simple. However, following examples from Italy and Germany, the doors are made as much 'in your face' as possible by the addition of metalwork, especially studding.

How will the doors be hinged or hung? The answer is that we are not hinging them all with metal. The evidence is that many Roman doors were hung on 'pivots', that is, a vertical pole of wood built in as an integral part of the door on the 'hinges' side. This has an extension top and bottom that fits into holes in the beams over the door and into the threshold across the bottom of the door. Examples also exist in stone where the pivot is eased in along a cut channel and kept in place with lead. But there are also iron hinges forged by blacksmiths.

Roman smiths were in many ways like 'modern' smiths. We know this from archaeology, pictures on tombs and the remains of tools. The Roman smith would have had a hearth on a platform to provide fire for heating iron. This would have been heated by charcoal (nowadays it is usually coke) with a double handled bellows to bring

Front doors from a reconstructed villa at Borg in Germany.

the temperature up. The tools for managing charcoal on the hearth have hardly altered, a shovel to put it on and a rake to move it around. The smiths dressed rather differently in Roman times and appears to have worn a one-sleeved tunic over the left shoulder in order to give the right arm the maximum amount of freedom. A major difference from today's smiths, who mostly work in what is known as 'mild steel', is that the Roman smiths would have been working in wrought iron.

Roman anvils were not like 'modern' ones: they are formed of a square block of iron less than one foot high splaying out from the base to the top and with the edges rounded. Some, but not all, have holes in the top to allow for punching holes in metal. This is done when an iron punch was hammered through hot soft metal. If the

A Roman blacksmith at work from the Catacomb of Domitilla, Rome.

158

punch hits the anvil top it will not form a proper hole – so a hole is left in the anvil to allow the punch to penetrate. Surviving Roman tools show a range of metal tongs to hold hot metal in the fire or grip it when it is being worked and there were a wide range of hammers from sledges to smaller ones. Cutting the metal seems to have always been done by punches or chisels as we know of no Roman equivalents to hacksaws. The use of lots of nails by the Romans has already been referred to and the Romans did have a specialised tool for making the heads of nails to make things easier for them. This was an iron bar expanded at one end which is pierced by a square or round tapering hole. The fact that the hole tapers is important. The nail is forged as a rod with one end made into a point. The other end is then dropped into the narrow end of the tapering hole, rested over the anvil and the protruding metal is hammered to forge the nail head. This is not very different from a technique that was used until fairly recently.

## IT'S CURTAINS FOR BUTSER

If there are not doors controlling access to entrances, especially internal ones, what else might have been there? How about curtains? It might seem surprising to us but curtains do seem to have played a significant role in this way but there is a problem in that curtains will not normally appear in the archaeological record because they can decay very easily. Surviving Roman curtains and curtain fragments only come from the desert conditions of Egypt which means that we can only speculate about the presence of curtains in Roman Britain. One way of approaching this topic is to look at the evidence in Roman doorways. The wood will have rotted, but if there is an absence of door 'furniture' – hinges, locks, studs and so on – perhaps there was a curtain? But as has been said before 'absence of evidence is not evidence of absence'. The ironwork might have been carried away or else rusted so thoroughly as to be unrecognisable or thought important. So archaeology does not really help us. We can turn to

sculpture and literature for assistance. In his description of the Gothic King Theodoric, dated to around AD 454, Sidonius describes the routine of his public life:

> *administrative duties . . . take up the rest of the morning. Armed nobles stand about the royal seat; the mass of guards in their garb of skins are admitted that they may be within call, but kept at the threshold for quiet's sake; only a murmur of them comes from their post at the doors, between the curtain and the outer barrier.*[1]

This is very much in the tradition of the morning *salutatio* that we considered when we were looking at the functions of the main reception/summer dining room. So why not have a curtain over the wide entrance to this room, to be closed at times so that the murmur of waiting clients could be heard in the corridor where they could not be seen? What better way to publicly demonstrate power and control?

Later Sidonius visits an old acquaintance called Maximus '*linked by old ties of hospitality*'[2] He makes the visit to plead for another friend who is very ill and being harassed by the bailiffs for repayment of a debt due to Maximus which is being charged at an interest of twelve per cent over ten years (which shows that our culture is not the first to experience problems with debt). Maximus, it becomes clear to Sidonius when he sees him and his villa, has become a Christian priest:

> *his dress, his walk, his humility, his pallor, his mode of speech – all declared the churchman. And then his hair was short and his beard long; he had simple tripod seats;* **coarse Cilician hangings covered his doors** [my emphasis]*; the beds were featherless, the tables unadorned.*[3]

'Cilician' describes rough fabrics made out of goat's hair – remember that they were thought suitable for throwing over the hurdles which

Roman-syle glassware as used for the feast at Butser in October 2003.

161

covered the temporary bathhouse/sauna in Chapter 4. The important point to be made here is that door curtains were common.

We get some help from sculpture and mosaics. The mosaic of the Empress Theodora, at the church of San Vitale in Ravenna, Italy, dated to around AD 547, shows a curtain in the background leading into a church. This is decorated with multicoloured rosettes and is pulled back to the left of the doorway in a knot. The way that curtains were held back by being tied in a knot features elsewhere. While this looks reasonable for a fine fabric (and we will come to those) I am not too sure about tying back the equivalent of thick woollen blankets in this fashion.

So while we have no archaeological evidence from Roman Britain for curtains, it would seem reasonable from the evidence outlined above to have them on some of the Butser villa doorways. But what sort? For the entrance from the ante-room to the kitchen/service room it would seem to be best to have something downmarket, coarse and heavy – we don't have Cilician goat's hair but the equivalent in heavy wool would seem to be appropriate. This leaves us with the wide entrances between the corridor and the reception/summer dining room and between the corridor and the ante-room to the 'private suite': these should have curtains of higher quality fabrics.

One largely complete example of a curtain from Egypt, now in the Royal Ontario Museum in Canada, is of linen with decoration in woolen tapestry weave principally in black, but also including red, orange, yellow, green and blue. There are eleven horizontal lines of motifs taken from hunt scenes such as horses, dogs, lions, deer, wild goats and hares. These are alternated in the lines with trees – with no attempt to give perspective but presumably to show the hunt environment. Other fragments of such curtains also seem to show hunt motifs. So this gives us on set of themes for decorating the higher status curtains.

Another way of decorating curtains comes from fragments in a Roman army rubbish dump also found in Egypt. To be fair we cannot be sure that they were curtains, equally they might be some sort of large spread. These were of flax with red and white, presumably vertical, stripes. The stripes are ten to fifteen millimetres apart and vary in width from less than ten millimetres to about twenty millimetres. The arrangement of stripes seemed to be entirely random. Another curtain (or spread) had blue and white stripes which seem much more regular and equal in width to each other. However, they do vary across the fabric – in one area ten to fifteen millimetres wide but elsewhere five to eight millimetres wide.

## CONSPICUOUS CONSUMPTION

In considering curtains we have started to move towards considering the 'symbolic' uses of the villa for expressions of social attitude so we will finish by considering the customs of dining.

To end on a note of excessive consumption we could turn to the excesses of Trimalchio's feast satirised by Petronius in his *Satyricon*. But instead let us turn to a person whom I hope by now is a sort of friend, namely Sidonius Apollinaris. What does Sidonius tell us about feasting and dining? Sometime in the AD 460's Sidonius is enjoying the hospitality of two friends (and he is related to both) somewhere near Nîmes in the south of France. After games and reading and while chatting:

*appears an envoy from the cook to warn us that the moment of bodily refreshment is at hand . . . The dinner was short, but*

Preparing Roman food for the Butser feast in October 2003.

*abundant served in the fashion affected in senatorial houses*
*where inveterate usage prescribes numerous courses on very*
*few dishes, though to afford variety, roast alternated with stew.*
*Amusing and instructive anecdotes accompanied our*
*potations.*[4]

For a rather more fraught occasion we have the description of a feast
to which he had been invited by the Emperor Majorian. This was a
very doubtful honour because Sidonius had been accused of writing

a vicious satire on Majorian and the main accuser was present at the
feast. Seating for the feast was on a horseshoe shaped set of couches
or single couch called the *stibandium*, with the open end facing into
the room. The Emperor, as host, sat on the right-hand end of the
*stibandium* and the main guest on the left-hand end. His name was
Severinus, consul for the year 'who managed to trim his sails to a
wind of even favour throughout our vast dynastic changes and
uneven fortunes of the State'. Next to him was Magnus, an ex-consul,

then Magnus's nephew, Camillus, who was also an ex-office holder. Then there was Paeonius, the person who was accusing Sidonius, then Athenius, 'a man versed in every turn of controversy and vicissitude of the times'. Next was Gratianensis, 'a character not to be mentioned in the same breath with evil, and though lower in rank than Severinus, above him in the imperial estimation'. Then comes Sidonius next to the Emperor! So Sidonius reclined next to the powerful person he was said to have satirised, one person away from his accuser. When the dinner is well under way the Emperor,

addressing his guests in order of importance, first talks with the consul, Severinus, then Magnus, exchanging literary remarks. He then moves his conversation to Camillus who makes a much applauded witty remark and then – 'by accident or set purpose, I cannot say which, the prince now passed over Paeonius and addressed some question to Athenius'. Paeonius takes this badly, interrupts Athenius, is 'rebuked' by a laugh from the Emperor, then Athenius, who is fuming because Paeonius has been placed in a

The completed front of Butser Roman villa, October 2002.

The build team and volunteers celebrate the completion of the villa on 4 October 2003.

superior position on the stibandium, is rude about Paeonius (still with me?). Gratianensis, the 'evil one', points out that this is worthy of a satirist which puts our Sidonius in the frame. There is an exchange with the Emperor in which it is agreed that Sidonius undertook 'to ask in an impromptu our sanction for writing satire' – Sidonius rapidly composed the following:

> *O mightiest prince, I pray that this be thy decree: let him who calls me libeller prove his charge or fear.*

Sidonius then modestly adds:

> *I do not want to seem conceited, but the applause which followed was equal to that which greeted Camillus; although it was earned, of course, less by the merit of the verse than by the speed with which I had composed.*[5]

The Emperor, having had his entertainment, forgives any charge against Sidonius, the rest of the dinner party who had been shunning him then greet him as they are putting on their mantles and Paeonius who had been 'frozen with terror' is forgiven.

OK, so we scale down the status of the company for the Butser Roman villa, but the arrangement of the couches and order of merit of the guests would be much the same. So the Butser Roman villa, like any other villa, expressed a concern with power, rank, status, and dependency. I wouldn't mind betting that there would be the same sort of jealousy, backbiting and rumours circulating among the clients and companions of the owner as there was in Sidonius's description. And perhaps it did not always end so triumphantly for the accused.

But let us end on a happier note. Sidonius also describes the setting of a feast. Again, it's on a grander scale than one which would have happened at Butser but it is what the owner of our villa would have liked to aspire to – one day:[6]

*Bring out the hangings of fine linen ruddy of hue . . . Let the fabric from a far land display the heights of Ctesiphon . . ., and the wild beasts racing over the field driven to madness by wounds skilfully feigned in red, from which a blood which is no blood seems to issue, as though a real dart had pierced their side. There the Parthian . . . vanishes on swift steed . . . putting in . . . flight the wild beasts' counterfeited forms. Let the round table be spread with linen purer than snow, and covered with laurel, with ivy and the green growths of the vine. Pile great baskets high (with flowers); let sideboard and couch be gay with garlands of sweet scent. Let some hands be perfumed with balsam smooth your disordered hair; let frankincense of Araby smoke to the lofty roof. Come the dark, let there be many a light be hung from the glittering ceiling high in the chamber's upper space. Let servitors bear in on laden shoulders food fit for kings, their necks bowed under silver richly chased . . .*

Back and side view of
the completed villa,
October 2003.

# BACK TO THE
# FUTURE

On Saturday 4 October 2003 the building of the villa was officially 'finished'. But of course it wasn't really finished – like any other building it never will be, although we can in all honesty say that the day marked the end of the beginning! Over the next month the villa was 'put to bed' for the late autumn and winter – memories of the weather conditions from the previous year are still very fresh, and we didn't want to be working on the structure, even inside, until the spring of 2004.

So what about the future? We have so much to learn from the villa reconstruction that it is difficult to know where to start. One thing that we will be looking for is the considered reaction of Roman experts rather than the first their impressions. We already know that there will be strongly felt views on some aspects of the villa and that they will be in total disagreement. My current favourite are the views expressed on the height of the 'winter dining room' which has a low ceiling. One Professor (and it is unfair to name names at this stage) was very happy that the ceiling was low because he felt that too much emphasis was put into reconstructing high-roofed rooms in Roman buildings and that many would have had low rooms. A plus to Butser! Two minutes afterwards another eminent expert said that the ceiling height was all wrong because the Romans went for rooms with high ceilings. A minus for Butser!  If two such people can disagree so fundamentally on such a basic point then it shows how much we have to learn, but because we have high and low rooms at Butser we can look at both aspects and see what practical considerations might come into play.

The first matter we will consider is how long the villa will take to dry out enough to become habitable. At the time of writing in autumn 2003, the amount of water in the fabric makes it a very chilly and raw experience to be inside for any length of time. So when spring comes it will be interesting to see how it feels. It will also be interesting to see how the wattle and daub dries out, the degree of cracking that we will experience and what happens to the wall-plaster and wall paintings. If we have a mild and wet winter will mould become a problem? And how long will it take for the *op.sig.* to dry properly and will it take a polish next year?

We are also interested in the amount of natural light that comes into the different rooms during the changing seasons and at different times of the day. We know that the summer dining room is flooded with light in the morning through the wide doorways, what is surprising is the effect that the high rear windows have in the afternoon and early evening in giving a back light. So morning sun for the *salutatio* and evening sun for the dinner.

When we used the kitchen/service room for cooking the 4 October 'feast' it was surprising how much smoke from the room spread throughout the rest of the villa into the higher status rooms, even with all the upper windows open. It makes a point about where cooking took place – so we will want to carefully look at the problem again. And here's another practical point – the cook found it really very tiresome not to have a drain or sump in the room. Is the room in fact a kitchen?

The real fun though will be considering the heating of the villa. The hypocaust should have dried out sufficiently by next spring for us to start firing it up properly, to see how much fuel and time is needed to bring it up to a reasonable heat, and then to maintain that heat. And of course, we will also find out how the heat from that room affects the surrounding ones. We were very impressed by the heat from the braziers and we will also be monitoring the heat that they produce, as well as the fumes. The first reaction is that they are seriously effective at heating rooms and we may need to rethink our attitude to Roman heating.

*Rebuilding the past: a Roman Villa* was a project with a fair number of problems, personal, practical and academic. For me, while it caused times of stress, it was also hugely enjoyable. Most importantly we now have a building – yes a villa – which will be there for a long time for the use, education and enjoyment of everybody from the oldest to the youngest from experts to the casual visitors. Why not come and see us at Butser Ancient Farm sometime and learn alongside us?

Guests enjoy the feast at Butser Roman villa, October 2003.

# NOTES

CHAPTER 1
1. Samuel Pepys, *The Shorter Pepys*, ed. R. Latham (Harmondsworth, Penguin, 1987) p. 295
2. ed. Alan Sorrell, *Reconstructing the Past* (London, Batsford, 1981) p.21.
3. Guy de la Bédoyère, *The Buildings of Roman Britain* (Stroud, Tempus, 2001) p.8.
4. David Mason, *Excavations at Chester: The Elliptical Building, an Image of the Roman World* (Chester, Chester City Council, 2000) p.6.

CHAPTER 2
1. The Younger Pliny, *Letters of the Younger Pliny*, tr. B. Radice (Harmondsworth, Penguin, 1963) pp.75–9.
2. Sidonius Apollinaris, *The Letters of Sidonius*, ed. O. M. Dalton (Oxford, OUP, 1915) pp.36–40.
3. W. H. Plommer, *Vitruvius and Later Roman Building Manuals* (CUP, 1973) p.41.

CHAPTER 3
1. Vitruvius Pollio, *The Ten Books on Architecture*, tr. I. G. Rowland, Commentary T. N. Howe (Cambridge University Press, 1999) p.76.

CHAPTER 4
1. Plommer, p.43.
2. de la Bédoyère, p.19.
3. Plommer, pp.73-4.
4. Gilbert White, *The Illustrated Natural History of Selborne*, Intro. J. E. Chatfield (Exeter, Webb & Bower, 1981) pp.139-40.
5. Vitruvius, p.42.
6. J. P. Adams, *Roman Building: materials and techniques*, tr. A Matthews (London, Batsford, 1994) p.70.

CHAPTER 5
1. Tacitus, *Tacitus on Britain and Germany*, tr. H. Matingly (Harmondsworth, Penguin, 1960) p.72.
2. Michael Jarrett, *Whitton: an Iron Age and Roman farmstead in South Glamorgan* (Cardiff, University of Wales Press, 1981) p.4.
3. Jarrett, p.253.
4. Sidonius, v.II, p.212.
5. Sidonius, v.I, p.52.
6. Sidonius, v.I, p.39
7. Sidonius. v.I, p.62

CHAPTER 6
1. Pliny, p.39.
2. Roger Ling, 'A collapsed building façade from Carsington, Derbyshire' *Britannia*, XXIII, (1992) pp.233–6.

CHAPTER 7
1. Vitruvius. p.110.
2. Vitruvius. p.96.
3. *The Mabinogion*, tr. G. Jones and T. Jones (London, J M Dent & Sons, 1975) pp.139–40.
4. Vitruvius, p.106.
5. Vitruvius, p.88.

CHAPTER 8
1. Plommer, p.73.
2. Plommer, p.75.
3. Plommer, p.73.
4. Roger Ling, *Roman Painting* (Cambridge University Press, 1991) p.220.

CHAPTER 9
1. Sidonius, Letters Vol I pp.3-4
2. Sidonius, Letters Vol II p.43.
3. Sidonius, Letters Vol II p.43.
4. Sidonius, Letters Vol I p.51.
5. Sidonius, Letters Vol I pp.30-3.
6. Sidonius, Letters Vol II p.203.

# FURTHER
# READING

If you want to find out what archaeological books have been recently published try the Society of Antiquaries Library website which can be found on www.sal.org.uk

Three good recent books to start with are . . .

**The Roman House in Britain** by Dominic Perring, Routledge, London 2002
*On the pricey side, this contains some interesting ideas, which are not accepted by everybody, and gives a good list of references – you won't want for more.*

**The Buildings of Roman Britain** by Guy de la Bédoyère, Tempus, Stroud, 2001
*Written by the ex-presenter of the The Discovery Channel's* Rebuilding the Past *series, this starts with an introduction to construction techniques and then has a challenging set of reconstruction drawings based on a variety of Roman sites.*

**Roman Buildings: Materials and Techniques** by Jean-Pierre Adam, translated by Anthony Mathews, Batsford, London, 1994
*This is based on a study of empire-wide material but is very good in giving the background.*

Some more specialist topic books include . . .

**Vitruvius: Ten Books on Architecture**, translated by I. G. Rowland with commentary by T. N. Howe, Cambridge University Press, Cambridge, 1999
*This is the most recent and accessible version of this classic Roman text.*

**Roman Painting** by Roger Ling, Cambridge University Press, Cambridge 1991
*A good overall introduction for mosaics. Or try . . .*

**Ancient Mosaics** by Roger Ling, British Museum Press, London, 1998

**Roman Brick and Tile** by Gerald Brodribb, Alan Sutton, Gloucester, 1987
*Gets down to the 'nitty gritty' of building materials used by the Romans.*

**A Guide to the Roman Remains in Britain** by Roger Wilson, 4th edition, Constable, London, 2002
*Good if you want to visit Roman sites in Britain (with a useful list of museum websites).*

**Life and Letters on the Roman Frontier** by Alan Bowman, British Museum Press, London, 1994
*If you really want to know what life was like on Hadrian's Wall read the Romans' own words.*

# INDEX

# PICTURE CREDITS

We are very pleased that nearly all the pictures in this book have been provided by people involved in the villa project. Photographs taken during the build come from John Warner, a volunteer at Butser Ancient Farm, and Johanna Schwartz, director and producer of the Discovery Channel's *Rebuilding the Past* series. Many of the archive photos come from Professor Roger Wilson who also takes part in the series and the pictures of Sparsholt Roman villa have been provided by David Johnston, the original excavator of that site. The original drawings are by Mel Bliss, a member of the build team and the blueprints are from Tim Concannon of Butser's Board of Trustees.

The build team
prepare to wattle
and daub,
September 2003.

DAI MORGAN EVANS is the General Secretary of the Society of Antiquaries and Chairman of the Board of Trustees of Butser Ancient Farm.

CHRISTINE SHAW is Director of Butser Ancient Farm.

ROGER JAMES is Executive Producer of the Discovery Channel's *Rebuilding the Past* series.

BUTSER ANCIENT FARM has open days for the public from March to September on the last weekend of the month and holds additional special events throughout the year. School parties are welcome, by appointment, at any time. To find out more please visit www.butser.org.uk